THE SEVEN PRINCIPLES OF MAN

THE SEVEN PRINCIPLES OF MAN

BY
ANNIE BESANT

ISBN: 978-81-212-1920-4 (HB)
First Published, 1892
Published, 2018
Published by

Gyan Publishing House
5, Ansari Road
Daryaganj, New Delhi-110002
Phone: 011-47034999, 9811692060
www.gyanbooks.com
E-mail: books@gyanbooks.com

Printed at: G. Print Process, Delhi.

PREFACE.

Few words are needed in sending this little book out into the world. It is the first of a series of Manuals designed to meet the public demand for a simple exposition of Theosophical teachings. Some have complained that our literature is at once too abstruse, too technical, and too expensive for the ordinary reader, and it is our hope that the present series may succeed in supplying what is a very real want. Theosophy is not only for the learned; it is for all. It may be that among those who in these little books catch their first glimpse of its teachings, there may be a few who will be led by them to penetrate more deeply into its philosophy, its science, and its religion, facing its abstruser problems with the student's zeal and the neophyte's ardour. But these Manuals are not written for the eager student whom no initial difficulties can daunt; they are written for the busy men and women of the work-a-day world, and seek to make plain some of the great truths that render life easier to bear and death easier to face. Written by servants of the Masters who are the Elder Brothers of our race, they can have no other object than to serve our fellow-men.

THE SEVEN PRINCIPLES OF MAN.

INQUIRERS attracted to Theosophy by its central doctrine of the brotherhood of man, and by the hopes which it holds out of wider knowledge and of spiritual growth, are apt to be repelled when they make their first attempt to come into closer acquaintance with it, by the to them strange and puzzling names which flow glibly from the lips of Theosophists in conference assembled. They hear a tangle of Âtmâ-Buddhi, Kâma-Manas, Triad, Devachan, and what not, and feel at once that for them Theosophy is far too abstruse a study. Yet they might have become very good Theosophists, had not their initial enthusiasm been quenched with the *douche* of Sanskrit terms. In the present manual the smoking flax shall be more tenderly treated, and but few Sanskrit names shall be flung in the face of the inquirer. As a matter of fact the use of these terms has become general among Theosophists because the English language has no equivalents for them, and a long and clumsy sentence has to be used in their stead if the idea is to be conveyed at all. The initial trouble of learning the names has been preferred to the continued trouble of using roundabout descriptive phrases—" Kâma," for instance, being shorter and more precise than " the passional and emotional part of our nature ".

Man according to the Theosophical teaching is a

seven-fold being, or, in the usual phrase, has a septenary constitution. Putting it in another way, man's nature has seven aspects, may be studied from seven different points of view, is composed of seven principles. The clearest and best way of all in which to think of man is to regard him as one, the Spirit or true Self; this belongs to the highest region of the universe, and is universal, the same for all; it is a ray of God, a spark from the divine fire. This is to become an individual, reflecting the divine perfection, a son that grows into the likeness of his father. For this purpose the Spirit, or true Self, is clothed in garment after garment, each garment belonging to a definite region of the universe, and enabling the Self to come into contact with that region, gain knowledge of it, and work in it. It thus gains experience, and all its latent potentialities are gradually drawn out into active powers. These garments, or sheaths, are distinguishable from each other both theoretically and practically. If a man be looked at clairvoyantly each is distinguishable by the eye, and they are separable each from each either during physical life or at death, according to the nature of any particular sheath. Whatever words may be used, the fact remains the same—that he is essentially seven-fold, an evolving being, part of whose nature has already been manifested, part remaining latent at present, so far as the vast majority of humankind are concerned. Man's consciousness is able to function through as many of these aspects as have been already evolved in him into activity.

This evolution, during the present cycle of human development, takes place on five out of the seven planes of nature. The two higher planes—the sixth and seventh—will not be reached, save in the most exceptional cases, by the men of this humanity in the present cycle, and they may therefore be left out of sight for our present purpose. As, however, some confusion has arisen as to the seven planes through differences of the nomenclature, two diagrams are given at the end of this treatise showing the seven planes as they exist in our division of the universe, in correspondence with the vaster planes of the universe as a whole, and also the subdivision of the five into seven, as they are represented in some of our literature. A "plane" is merely a condition, a stage, a state; so that we might describe man as fitted by his nature, when that nature is fully developed, to exist consciously in seven different conditions, or seven different stages, in seven different states; or, technically, on seven different planes of being. To take an easily verified illustration: a man may be conscious on the physical plane, that is, in his physical body, feeling hunger and thirst, the pain of a blow or cut. But let the man be a soldier in the heat of battle, and his consciousness will be centred in his passions and emotions, and he may suffer a wound without knowing it, his consciousness being away from the physical plane and acting on the plane of passions and emotions: when the excitement is over, consciousness will pass back to the physical, and he will "feel" the pain of his wound. Let the man be a philosopher, and as he ponders over some knotty problem he will lose all consciousness of bodily wants, of emotions, of love and hatred; his consciousness will have passed to the plane of intellect, he will be "abstracted," *i.e.*, drawn away from considerations pertaining to his bodily life, and fixed on the plane of thought. Thus may a man live on these several planes, in these several conditions, one part or another of his nature being thrown into activity at any given time; and an understanding of what man is, of his nature, his powers, his possibilities, will be reached more easily and assimilated more usefully if he is studied along these clearly defined lines, than if he be left without analysis, a mere confused bundle of qualities and states.

It has also been found convenient, having regard to man's mortal and immortal life, to put these seven principles into two groups—one containing the three higher principles and therefore called the Triad, the other containing the four lower and therefore called the Quaternary. The Triad is the deathless part of man's nature, the "spirit" and soul of Christian terminology; the Quaternary is the mortal part, the "body" of Christianity. This division into body, soul, and spirit is used by St. Paul, and is recognized in all careful Christian philosophy, although generally ignored by the mass of Christian people. In ordinary parlance soul and body or spirit and body make up the man, and the words soul and spirit are used interchangeably, with much confusion of thought as the result. This looseness is fatal to any clear view of the constitution of man, and the Theosophist may well appeal to the Christian philosopher as against the casual Christian non-thinker if it be urged that he is making distinctions difficult to be grasped. No philosophy worthy of the name can be stated even in the most elementary fashion without making some demand on the intelligence and the attention of the would-be learner, and carefulness in the use of terms is a condition of all knowledge.

Principle I. The Dense Physical Body.

The dense physical body of man is called the first of his seven principles, as it is certainly the most obvious. Built of material molecules, in the generally accepted sense of the term, with its five organs of sensation—the five senses—its organs of locomotion, its brain and nervous system, its apparatus for carrying on the various functions necessary for its continued existence, there is little to be said about this physical body in so slight a sketch as this of the constitution of man. Western science is almost ready to accept the Theosophical view that the human organism consists of innumerable "lives," which build up the cells. H. P. Blavatsky says on this: "Science has never yet gone so far as to assert with the Occult doctrine that our bodies, as well as those of animals, plants, and stones, are themselves altogether built up of such beings [bacteria, etc.]: which, with the exception of the larger species, no microscope can detect. . . . The physical and chemical constituents of all being found to be identical, chemical science may well say that there is no difference between the matter which composes the ox and that which forms the man. But the Occult doctrine is far more explicit. It says: Not only the chemical compounds are the same, but the same infinitesimal *invisible* lives compose the atoms of the bodies of the mountain and the daisy, of man and the ant, of the elephant and of the tree which shelters him from the sun. Each particle—whether you call it organic or inorganic—*is a* life. Every atom and molecule in the universe is both *life-giving* and *death-giving* to such forms" (*Secret Doctrine*, vol. i., p. 281, new edition). The microbes thus "build up the material body and its cells," under the constructive energy of vitality—a phrase that will be explained when we come to deal with "life," as the Third Principle, and with these microbes as part of it. When the "life" is no longer supplied the microbes "are left to run riot as destructive agents," and they break up and disintegrate the cells which they built, and so the body goes to pieces.

The purely physical consciousness is the consciousness of the cells and the molecules. The selective action of the cells, taking from the blood what they need, rejecting what they do not need, is an instance of this self-consciousness. The process goes on without the help of our consciousness or volition. Again that which is called by physiologists unconscious memory is the memory of this physical consciousness, unconscious to us indeed, until we have learned to transfer our brain-consciousness thither. What we feel is not what the cells feel. The *pain* of a wound is felt by the brain-consciousness, acting, as before said, on the physical plane; but the consciousness of the molecule, as of the aggregation of molecules we call cells, leads it to hurry to the repair of the damaged tissues—actions of which the brain is *un*conscious—and its memory makes it repeat the same act again and again, even when it has become unnecessary. Hence cicatrices on wounds, scars, callosities, etc. The student may find many details on this subject in physiological treatises.

The death of the dense physical body occurs when the withdrawal of the controlling life-energy leaves the microbes to go their own way, and the many lives, no longer co-ordinated, separate from each other and scatter thc particles of the cells of "the man of dust," and what we call decay sets in. The body becomes a whirlpool of unrestrained, unregulated lives, and its form, which resulted from their corrclation, is destroyed by their exuberant individual encrgy. Death is but an aspect of life, and the destruction of one material form is but a prelude to the building up of another.

Principle II. The Etheric Double.

The Linga Sharîra, the astral body, the ethereal body, the fluidic body, the double, the wraith, the döppelganger, the astral man—such are a few of the many names which have been given to the second principle in man's constitution. The best name is the Etheric Double, because this term designates the second principle only, suggesting its constitution and appearance: whereas the other names have been used somewhat generally to describe bodies formed of more subtle matter than that which affects our physical senses, without regard to the question whether other principles were or were not involved in their construction. I shall therefore use this name throughout.

The etheric double is formed of matter rarer or more subtle than that which is perceptible to our five senses, but still matter belonging to the physical plane, to which its functioning is confined. It is the state of physical matter which is just beyond our "solid, liquid, and gas," which form the dense portions of the physical plane.

This etheric double is the exact double or counterpart of the dense physical body to which it belongs, and is separable from it, although unable to go very far away therefrom. In normal healthy human beings the separation is a matter of difficulty, but in persons known as physical or materializing mediums, the ethereal double slips out without any great effort. When separated from the dense body it is visible to the clairvoyant as an exact replica thereof, united to it by a slender thread. So close is the physical union between the two that an injury inflicted on the etheric double appears as a lesion on the dense body, a fact known under the name of repercussion. A. d'Assier, in his well-known work—translated by Colonel H. S. Olcott, the President-Founder of the Theosophical Society, under the title of *Posthumous Humanity*—gives a number of cases (see pp. 51-57) in which this repercussion took place.

Separation of the etheric double from the dense body is generally accompanied by a considerable decrease of vitality in the latter, the double becoming more vitalized as the energy in the dense body diminishes. Colonel Olcott says in a note in the book just mentioned (p. 63):—

"When the double is projected by a trained expert, even, the body seems torpid, and the mind in a 'brown study' or dazed state; the eyes are lifeless in expression, the heart and lung actions feeble, and often the temperature much lowered. It is very dangerous to make any sudden noise, or burst into the room, under such circumstances; for the double being by instantaneous reaction drawn back into the body, the heart convulsively palpitates, and death even may be caused."

In the case of Emilie Sagée (quoted on pp. 62-65), the girl was noticed to look pale and exhausted when the double was visible: "the more distinct the double and more material in appearance, the really material person was proportionately wearied, suffering and languid; when, on the contrary, the appearance of the double weakened, the patient was seen to recover strength". This phenomenon is perfectly intelligible to the Theosophical student, who knows that the etheric double is the vehicle of the life-principle, or vitality, in the physical body, and that its partial withdrawal must therefore diminish the energy with which this principle plays on the denser molecules.

Clairvoyants, such as the Seeress of Prevorst, state that they can see the ethereal arm or leg attached to a body from which the dense limb has been amputated, and D'Assier remarks on this:—

> "Whilst I was absorbed in physiological studies, I was often arrested by a singular fact. It sometimes happens that a person who has lost an arm or leg experiences certain sensations at the extremities of the fingers or toes. Physiologists explain this anomaly by postulating in the patient an inversion of sensitiveness or of recollection, which makes him locate in the hand or the foot the sensation with which the nerve of the stump is alone affected. . . . I confess that these explanations seemed to me laboured and have never satisfied me. When I studied the problem of the duplication of man, the question of amputations recurred to my mind, and I asked myself if it was not more simple and logical to attribute the anomaly of which I have spoken to the doubling of the human body, which by its fluidic nature can escape amputation" (*loc. cit.*, pp. 103, 104).

The etheric double plays a great part in spiritualistic phenomena. Here again the clairvoyant can help us. A clairvoyant can see the etheric double oozing out of the left side of the medium, and it is this which often appears as the "materialized spirit," easily moulded into various shapes by the thought-currents of the sitters, and gaining strength and vitality as the medium sinks into a deep trance. The Countess Wachtmeister, who is clairvoyant, says that she has seen the same "spirit" recognized as that of a near relative or friend by different sitters, each of whom saw it according to his expectations, while to her own eyes it was the mere double of the medium. So again H. P. Blavatsky told me that when she was at the Eddy homestead, watching the remarkable series of phenomena there produced, she deliberately moulded the "spirit" that appeared into the likenesses of persons known to herself and to no one else present, and the other sitters saw the types which she produced by her own will-power, moulding the plastic matter of the medium's etheric double.

Many of the movements of objects that occur at such séances, and at other times, without visible contact, are due to the action of the etheric double, and the student can learn how to produce such phenomena at will. They are trivial enough: the mere putting out of the etheric hand is no more important than the putting out of the dense counterpart, and neither more nor less miraculous. Some persons produce such phenomena unconsciously, mere aimless overturnings of objects, making of noises, and so on: they have no control over their etheric double, and it just blunders about in their near neighbourhood, like a baby trying to walk. For the etheric double, like the dense body, has only a diffused consciousness belonging to its parts, and has no mentality. Nor does it readily serve as a medium of mentality, when disjoined from the dense counterpart.

This leads us to an interesting point. The centres of sensation are located in the fourth principle, which may be said to form the bridge between the physical organs and the mental perceptions; impressions from the physical universe impinge on the material molecules of the dense physical body, setting in vibration the constituent cells of the organs of sensations, or our "senses". These vibrations, in their turn, set in motion the finer material molecules of the etheric double, in the corresponding sense organs of its finer matter. From these the vibrations pass to the astral body, or fourth principle, presently to be considered, wherein are the corresponding centres of sensation. From these vibrations are again propagated into the yet rarer matter of the lower mental plane, whence they are reflected back until, reaching the material molecules of the cerebral hemispheres, they become our "brain-consciousness". This correlated and unconscious succession is necessary for the normal action of consciousness as we know it. In sleep and in trance, natural or induced, the first two and the last stages are generally omitted, and the impressions start from and return to the astral plane, and thus make no trace on the brain-memory; but the natural or trained psychic, the clairvoyant who does not need trance for the exercise of his powers, is able to transfer his consciousness from the physical to the astral plane without losing grip thereof, and can impress the brain-memory with knowledge gained on the astral plane, so retaining it for use.

Death means for the etheric double just what it means for the dense physical body, the breaking up of its constituent parts, the dissipation of its molecules. The vehicle of the vitality that animates the bodily organism as a whole, it oozes forth from the body when the death-hour comes, and is seen by the clairvoyant as a violet light, or violet form, hovering over the dying person, still attached to the physical body by the slender thread before spoken of. When the thread snaps, the last breath has quivered outwards, and the bystanders whisper "He is dead".

The etheric double, being of physical matter, remains in the neighbourhood of the corpse, and is the "wraith," or "apparition," or "phantom," sometimes seen at the moment of death and afterwards by persons near the place where the death has occurred. It disintegrates slowly *pari passu* with its dense counterpart, and its remnants are seen by sensitives in cemeteries and churchyards as violet lights hovering over graves. Here is one of the reasons which render cremation preferable to burial as a mode of disposing of the physical envelopes of man ; the fire dissipates in a few hours the molecules which would otherwise be set free only in the slow course of gradual putrefaction, and thus quickly restores to their own plane the dense and etheric materials, ready for use once more in the building up of new forms.

Principle III. Prâna, the Life.

All universes, all worlds, all men, all brutes, all vegetables, all minerals, all molecules and atoms, all that *is*, are plunged in a great ocean of life, life eternal, life infinite, life incapable of increase or of diminution. The universe is only life in manifestation, life made objective, life differentiated. Now each organism, whether minute as a molecule or vast as a universe, may be thought of as appropriating to itself somewhat of life, of embodying in itself as its own life some of this universal life. Figure a living sponge, stretching itself out in the water which bathes it, envelops it, permeates it; there is water, still the ocean, circulating in every passage, filling every pore; but we may think of the ocean outside the sponge, or of the part of the ocean appropriated by the sponge, distinguishing them in thought if we want to make statements about each severally. So each organism is a sponge bathed in the ocean of life universal, and containing within itself some of that ocean as its own breath of life. In Theosophy we distinguish this appropriated life under the name Prâna, breath, and call it the third principle in man's constitution.

To speak quite accurately, the "breath of life"—that which the Hebrews termed *Nephesch*, or the breath of life breathed into the nostrils of Adam—is not Prâna only, but Prâna and the fourth principle conjoined. It is these two together that make the "vital spark"

(*Secret Doctrine*, vol. i., p. 262), and that are the "breath of life in man, as in beast or insect, of physical, material life" (*ibid.*, note to p. 263). It is "the breath of animal life in man—the breath of life instinctual in the animal" (*ibid.*, diagram on p. 262). But just now we are concerned with Prâna only, with vitality as the animating principle in all animal and human bodies. Of this life the etheric double is the vehicle, acting, so to say, as means of communication, as bridge, between Prâna and the dense body.

Prâna is explained in the *Secret Doctrine* as having for its lowest subdivision the microbes of science; these are the "invisible lives" that build up the physical cells (see *ante*, pp. 8, 9); these are the "countless myriads of lives" that build the "tabernacle of clay," the physical bodies (*Secret Doctrine*, vol. i., p. 245). "Science, dimly perceiving the truth, may find bacteria and other infinitesimals in the human body, and see in them only occasional and abnormal visitors to which diseases are attributed. Occultism—which discerns a life in every atom and molecule, whether in a mineral or human body, in air, fire, or water—affirms that our whole body is built of such lives; the smallest bacterium under the microscope being to them in comparative size like an elephant to the tiniest infusoria" (*ibid.*, p. 245). The "fiery lives" are the controllers and directors of these microbes, these invisible lives, and "indirectly" build, *i.e.*, build by controlling and directing the microbes, the immediate builders, supplying the latter with what is necessary, acting as the life of these lives: the "fiery lives," the synthesis, the essence, of Prâna, are the "vital constructive energy" that enables the microbes to build the physical cells. One of the archaic commentaries sums up the matter in stately and luminous phrases: "The worlds, to the profane, are built up of the known elements. To the conception of an Arhat, these elements are themselves collectively a divine life; distributively, on the plane of manifestations, the numberless and countless crores* of lives. Fire alone is ONE, on the plane of the One Reality; on that of manifested, hence illusive, being, its particles are fiery lives which live and have their being at the expense of every other life that they consume. Therefore they are named the Devourers. . . . Every visible thing in this universe was built by such lives, from conscious and divine primordial man, down to the unconscious agents that construct matter. . . . From the One Life, formless and uncreate, proceeds the universe of lives" (*Secret Doctrine*, vol. i., p. 269). As in the universe, so in man, and all these countless lives, all this constructive vitality, all this is summed up by the Theosophist as Prâna.

* A crore is ten millions.

Principle IV. The Desire-Body.

In building up our man we have now reached the principle sometimes described as the animal soul, in Theosophical parlance Kâma Rûpa, or the desire-body. It belongs to in constitution, and functions on, the second or astral plane. It includes the whole body of appetites, passions, emotions, and desires which come under the head of instincts, sensations, feelings and emotions, in our Western psychological classification, and are dealt with as a subdivision of mind. In Western psychology mind is divided—by the modern school—into three main groups, feelings, will, intellect. Feelings are again divided into sensations and emotions, and these are divided and subdivided under numerous heads. Kâma, or desire, includes the whole group of "feelings," and might be described as our passional and emotional nature. All animal needs, such as hunger, thirst, sexual desire, come under it; all passions, such as love (in its lower sense), hatred, envy, jealousy. It is the desire for sentient existence, for experience of material joys—"the lust of the flesh, the lust of the eyes, the pride of life". This principle is the most material in our nature, it is the one that binds us fast to earthly life. "It is not molecularly constituted matter, least of all the human body, Sthûla Sharira, that is the grossest of all our 'principles,' but verily the *middle* principle, the real animal centre; whereas our body is but its shell, the irresponsible factor and medium through which the beast in us acts all its life" (*Secret Doctrine*, vol. i., pp. 280, 281).

United to the lower part of Manas, the mind, as Kâma-Manas, it becomes the normal human brain-intelligence, and that aspect of it will be dealt with presently. Considered by itself, it remains the brute in us, the "ape and tiger" of Tennyson, the force which most avails to keep us bound to earth and to stifle in us all higher longings by the illusions of sense.

Kâma joined to Prâna is, as we have seen, the "breath of life," the vital sentient principle spread over every particle of the body. It is, therefore, the seat of sensation, that which enables the organs of sensation to function. We have already noted that the physical organs of sense, the bodily instruments that come into immediate contact with the external world, are related to the organs of sensation in the etheric double (*ante*, p. 14). But these organs would be incapable of functioning did not Prâna make them vibrant with activity, and their vibrations would remain vibrations only, motion on the material plane of the physical body, did not Kâma, the principle of sensation, translate the vibration into feeling. Feeling, indeed, is consciousness on the kâmic plane, and when a man is under the dominion of a sensation or a passion, the Theosophist speaks of him as on the kâmic plane, meaning thereby that his consciousness is functioning on that plane. For instance, a tree may reflect rays of light, that is ethereal vibrations, and these vibrations striking on the outer eye will set up vibrations in the physical nerve-cells; these will be propagated as vibrations to the physical and on to the astral centres, but there is no *sight* of the tree until the seat of sensation is reached, and Kâma enables us to *perceive*.

Matter of the astral plane—including that called elemental essence—is the material of which the desire-body is composed, and it is the peculiar properties of this matter which enable it to serve as the sheath in which the Self can gain experience of sensation. (The constitution of the elemental essence would lead us too far from an elementary treatise.) The desire-body, or astral body, as it is often called, has the form of a mere cloudy mass during the earlier stages of evolution, and is incapable of serving as an independent vehicle of consciousness. During deep sleep it escapes from the physical body, but remains near it, and the mind within it is almost as much asleep as the body. It is, however, liable to be affected by forces of the astral plane akin to its own constitution, and gives rise to dreams of a sensuous kind. In a man of average intellectual development the desire-body has become more highly organized, and when separated from the physical body is seen to resemble it in outline and features; even then, however, it is not conscious of its surroundings on the astral plane, but encloses the mind as a shell, within which the mind may actively function, while not yet able to use it as an independent vehicle of consciousness. Only in the highly evolved man does the desire-body become thoroughly organized and vitalized, as much the vehicle of conscious ness on the astral plane as the physical body is on the physical plane.

After death, the higher part of man dwells for awhile in the desire-body, the length of its stay depending on the comparative grossness or delicacy of its constituents. When the man escapes from it, it persists for a time as a " shell," and when the departed entity is of a low type, and during earth-life infused such mentality as it possessed into the passional nature, some of this remains entangled with the shell. It then possesses consciousness of a very low order, has brute cunning, is without conscience—an altogether objectional entity, often spoken of as a "spook". It strays about, attracted to all places in which animal desires are encouraged and satisfied, and is drawn into the currents of those whose animal passions are strong and unbridled. Mediums of low type inevitably attract these eminently undesirable visitors, whose fading vitality is reinforced in their séance-rooms, who catch astral reflections, and play the part of "disembodied spirits" of a low order. Nor is this all: if at such a séance there be present some man or woman of correspondingly low development, the spook will be attracted to that person, and may attach itself to him or to her, and thus may be set up currents between the desire-body of the living person and the dying desire-body of the dead person, generating results of the most deplorable kind.

The longer or shorter persistence of the desire-body as a shell or a spook depends on the greater or less development of the animal and passional nature in the dying personality. If during earth-life the animal nature was indulged and allowed to run riot, if the intellectual and spiritual parts of man were neglected or stifled, then, as the life-currents were set strongly in the direction of passion, the desire-body will persist for a long period after the body of the person is dead. Or again, if earth-life has been suddenly cut short by accident or by suicide, the link between Kâma and Prâna will not be easily broken, and the desire-body will be strongly vivified. If, on the other hand, desire has been conquered and bridled during earth-life, if it has been purified and trained into subservience to man's higher nature, then there is but little to energize the desire-body and it will quickly disintegrate and dissolve away.

There remains one other fate, terrible in its possibilities, which may befall the fourth principle, but it cannot be clearly understood until the fifth principle has been dealt with.

THE QUATERNARY, OR FOUR LOWER PRINCIPLES.

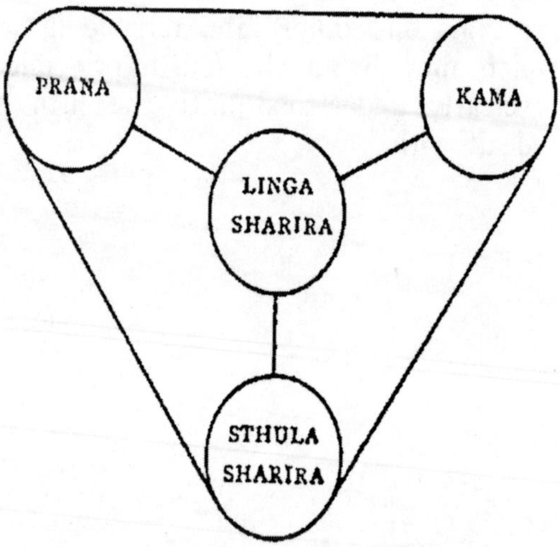

Diagram of the Quaternary; transitory and mortal: see Secret Doctrine, *vol. i., p.* 262.*

We have thus studied man, as to his lower nature, and have reached the point in his path of evolution to which

* The etheric double is here named the Linga Sharîra, a name now discarded in consequence of the confusion caused by employing a well-known term of Hindu philosophy in an entirely new sense. Before her departure H. P. B. urged her pupils to reform the terminology, which had been too carelessly put together, and we are trying to carry out her wish.

he is accompanied by the brute. The quaternary, regarded alone, ere it is affected by contact with the mind, is merely a lower animal; it awaits the coming of the mind to make it man. Theosophy teaches that through past ages man was thus slowly builded up, stage by stage, principle by principle, until he stood as a quaternary, brooded over but not in contact with the Spirit, waiting for that mind which could alone enable him to progress farther, and to come into conscious union with the Spirit, so fulfilling the very object of his being. This æonian evolution, in its slow progression, is hurried through in the personal evolution of each human being, each principle which was in the course of ages successively evolved in man on earth, appearing as part of the constitution of each man at the point of evolution reached at any given time, the remaining principles being latent, awaiting their gradual manifestation. The evolution of the quaternary until it reached the point at which further progress was impossible without mind, is told in eloquent sentences in the archaic stanzas on which the *Secret Doctrine* of H. P. Blavatsky is based (*breath* is the Spirit, for which the human tabernacle is to be builded; the *gross body* is the dense physical body; the *spirit of life* is Prâna; the *mirror of its body* is the etheric double; the *vehicle of desires* is Kâma):—

"The Breath needed a form; the Fathers gave it. The Breath needed a gross body; the Earth moulded it. The Breath needed the Spirit of Life; the Solar Lhas breathed it into its form. The Breath needed a Mirror of its Body; 'We gave it our own,' said the Dhyânis. The Breath needed a Vehicle of Desires; 'It has it,' said the Drainer of Waters. But Breath needs a Mind to embrace the Universe; 'We cannot give that,' said the Fathers. 'I never had it,' said the Spirit of the

Earth. 'The form would be consumed were I to give it mine,' said the Great Fire. . . . Man remained an empty senseless Bhûta" (phantom).

And so is the personal man without mind. The quaternary alone is not man, the Thinker, and it is as Thinker that man is really man.

Yet at this point let the student pause, and reflect over the human constitution, so far as he has gone. For this quaternary is the mortal part of man, and is distinguished by Theosophy as the *personality*. It needs to be very clearly and definitely realized, if the constitution of man is to be understood, and if the student is to read more advanced treatises with intelligence. True, to make the personality *human* it has yet to come under the rays of mind, and to be illuminated by it as the world by the rays of the sun. But even without these rays it is a clearly defined entity, with its dense body, its etheric double, its life, and its desire-body, or animal soul. It has passions, but no reason: it has emotions, but no intellect: it has desires, but no rationalized will: it awaits the coming of its monarch, the mind, the touch which shall transform it into man.

PRINCIPLE V. MANAS, THE THINKER, OR MIND.

We have reached the most complicated part of our study, and some thought and attention are necessary from the reader to gain even an elementary idea of the relation held by the fifth principle to the other principles in man.

The word Manas comes from the Sanskrit word *man*, the root of the verb to think; it is the Thinker in us, spoken of vaguely in the West as mind. I will ask the reader to regard Manas as Thinker rather than as mind, because the word Thinker suggests some one who thinks, *i.e.*, an individual, an entity. And this is exactly the Theosophical idea of Manas, for Manas is the immortal individual, the real "I," that clothes itself over and over again in transient personalities, and itself endures for ever. It is described in the *Voice of the Silence* in the exhortation addressed to the candidate for initiation: "Have perseverance as one who doth for evermore endure. Thy shadows [personalities] live and vanish; that which in thee shall live for ever, that which in thee *knows*, for it is knowledge, is not of fleeting life; it is the man that was, that is, and will be, for whom the hour shall never strike" (p. 31). H. P. Blavatsky has described it very clearly in the *Key to Theosophy*: "Try to imagine a 'Spirit,' a celestial being, whether we call it by one name or another, divine in its essential nature, yet not pure enough to be one with the ALL, and having, in order to achieve this, to so purify its nature as finally to gain that goal. It can do so only by passing *individually* and *personally*, *i.e.*, spiritually and physically, through every experience and feeling that exists in the manifold or differentiated universe. It has, therefore, after having gained such experience in the lower kingdoms, and having ascended higher and still higher with every rung on the ladder of being, to pass through every experience on the human planes. In its very essence it is Thought, and is, therefore, called in its plurality *Mânasaputra*, 'the Sons of (universal) Mind'. This *individualized* 'Thought' is what we Theosophists call the *real* human Ego, the thinking entity imprisoned in a case of flesh and bones. This is surely a spiritual entity, not *matter*,* and such entities are the incarnating Egos that inform the bundle of animal matter called mankind, and whose names are *Manasa* or minds" (*Key to Theosophy*, pp. 183, 184).

This idea may be rendered yet clearer perhaps by a hurried glance cast backward over man's evolution in the past. When the quaternary had been slowly built up, it was a fair house without a tenant, and stood empty awaiting the coming of the one who was to dwell therein. The name Mânasaputra (the sons of mind) covers many grades of intelligences, ranging from the mighty "Sons of the Flame" whose human evolution lies far behind them, down to those entities who gained individualization in the cycle preceding our own, and were ready to incarnate on this earth in order to accomplish their human stage of evolution. Some superhuman intelli-

* That is, not matter as we know it, on the plane of the objective universe.

gences incarnated as guides and teachers of our infant humanity, and became founders and divine rulers of the ancient civilizations. Large numbers of the entities spoken of above, who had already evolved some mental faculties, took up their abode in the human quaternary, in the mindless men. These are the reincarnating Mânasaputra, who became the tenants of the human frames as then evolved on earth, and these same Mânasaputra, reincarnating age after age, are the Reincarnating Egos, the Manas in us, the persistent individual, the fifth principle in man. The remainder of mankind through successive ages received from the loftier Mânasaputra their first spark of mind, a ray which stimulated into growth the germ of mind latent within them, the human soul thus having its birth in time there. It is these differences of age, as we may call them, in the beginning of the individual life, of the specialization of the eternal Divine Spirit into a human soul, which explain the enormous differences in mental capacity found in our present humanity.

The multiplicity of names given to this fifth principle has probably tended to increase the confusion surrounding it in the minds of many who are beginning to study Theosophy. *Mânasaputra* is what we may call the historical name, the name that suggests the entrance into humanity of a class of already individualized souls at a certain point of evolution; *Manas* is the ordinary name, descriptive of the intellectual nature of the principle; the *Individual* or the "*I*," or *Ego*, recalls the fact that this principle is permanent, does not die, is the individualizing principle, separating itself in thought from all that is not itself, the *Subject* in Western terminology as opposed to the *Object;* the *Higher Ego* puts it into contrast with the *Personal Ego*, of which something is to be presently said; the *Reincarnating Ego* lays stress on the fact that it is the principle that reincarnates continually, and so unites in its own experience all the lives passed through on earth. There are various other names, but they will not be met with in elementary treatises. The above are those most often encountered, and there is no real difficulty about them, but when they are used interchangeably, without explanation, the unhappy student is apt to tear his hair in anguish, wondering how many principles he has got hold of, and what relation they bear to each other.

We must now consider Manas during a single incarnation, which will serve as the type of all, and we will start when the Ego has been drawn—by causes set a-going in previous earth-lives—to the family in which is to be born the human being who is to serve as its next tabernacle. (I do not deal here with reincarnation, since that great and most essential doctrine of Theosophy must be expounded separately.) The Thinker, then, awaits the building of the "house of life" which he is to occupy: and now arises a difficulty; himself a spiritual entity living on the mental or third plane upwards, a plane far higher than that of the physical universe, he cannot influence the molecules of gross matter of which his dwelling is builded by the direct play upon them of his own most subtle particles. So he projects part of his own substance, which clothes itself with astral matter, and then with the help of etheric matter permeates the whole nervous system of the yet unborn child, to form, as the physical apparatus matures, the thinking principle in man. This projection from Manas, spoken of as its reflection, its shadow, its ray, and by many another descriptive and allegorical name, is the lower Manas, in contradistinction to the higher Manas—Manas, during every period of incarnation, being dual. On this, H. P. Blavatsky says: "Once imprisoned, or incarnate, their (the Manasa) essence becomes dual; that is to say the *rays* of the eternal divine Mind, considered as individual entities, assume a two-fold attribute which is (*a*) their essential, inherent, characteristic, heaven-aspiring mind (higher Manas), and (*b*) the human quality of thinking, or animal cogitation, rationalized owing to the superiority of the human brain, the Kâma-tending or lower Manas" (*Key to Theosophy*, p. 184).

We must now turn our attention to this lower Manas alone, and see the part which it plays in the human constitution.

It is engulfed in the quaternary, and we may regard it as clasping Kâma with one hand, while with the other it retains its hold on its father, the higher Manas. Whether it will be dragged down by Kâma altogether and be torn away from the triad to which by its nature it belongs, or whether it will triumphantly carry back to its source the purified experiences of its earth-life—that is the life-problem set and solved in each successive incarnation. During earth-life, Kâma and the lower Manas are joined together, and are often spoken of conveniently as Kâma-Manas. Kâma supplies, as we have seen, the animal and passional elements; the lower Manas rationalizes these, and adds the intellectual faculties; and so we have the brain-mind, the brain-intelligence, *i.e.*, Kâma-Manas functioning in the brain and nervous system, using the physical apparatus as its organ on the material plane. In man these two principles are interwoven during life, and rarely act separately, but the student must realize that "Kâma-Manas" is not a new principle, but the interweaving of the fourth with the lower part of the fifth.

As with a flame we may light a wick, and the colour of the flame of the burning wick will depend on the nature of the wick and of the liquid in which it is soaked, so in each human being the flame of Manas sets alight the brain and kâmic wick, and the colour of the light from that wick will depend on the kâmic nature and the development of the brain-apparatus. If the kâmic nature be strong and undisciplined it will soil the pure manasic light, lending it a lurid tinge and fouling it with noisome smoke. If the brain-apparatus be imperfect or undeveloped, it will dull the light and prevent it from shining forth to the outer world. As was clearly stated by H. P. Blavatsky in her article on "Genius": "What we call 'the manifestations of genius' in a person are only the more or less successful efforts of that Ego to assert itself on the outward plane of its objective form—the man of clay—in the matter-of-fact daily life of the latter. The Egos of a Newton, an Æschylus, or a Shakespeare are of the same essence and substance as the Egos of a yokel, an ignoramus, a fool, or even an idiot; and the self-assertion of their informing *genii* depends on the physiological and material construction of the physical man. No Ego differs from another Ego in its primordial or original essence and nature. That which makes of one mortal a great man, and of another a vulgar silly person is, as said, the quality and make-up of the physical shell or casing, and the adequacy or inadequacy of brain and body to transmit and give expression to the light of the real *inner* man; and this aptness or inaptness is, in its turn, the result of Karma. Or, to use another simile, physical man is the musical instrument, and the Ego the performing artist. The potentiality of perfect melody of sound is in the former—the instrument—and no skill of the latter can awaken a faultless harmony out of a broken or badly made instrument. This harmony depends on the fidelity of transmission, by word and act, to the objective plane, of the unspoken divine thought in the very depths of man's subjective or inner nature. Physical man may—to follow our simile—be a priceless Stradivarius, or a cheap and cracked fiddle, or again a mediocrity between the two, in the hands of the Paganini who ensouls him" (*Lucifer* for November, 1889, p. 228).

Bearing in mind these limitations and idiosyncrasies * imposed on the manifestations of the thinking principle by the organ through which it has to function, we shall have little difficulty in following the workings of the lower Manas in man ; mental ability, intellectual strength, acuteness, subtlety—all these are its manifestations ; these may reach as far as what is often called genius, what H. P. Blavatsky speaks of as "artificial genius, the outcome of culture and of purely intellectual acuteness". Its nature is often demonstrated by the presence of kâmic elements in it, of passion, vanity and arrogance.

The higher Manas can but rarely manifest itself at the present stage of human evolution. Occasionally a flash from those loftier regions lightens the twilight in which we dwell, and such flashes alone are what the Theosophist calls true genius: "Behold in every manifestation of genius, *when combined with virtue*, the undeniable presence of the celestial exile, the divine Ego whose jailer thou art, O man of matter". For Theosophy teaches "that the presence in man of various creative powers—called genius in their collectivity—is

* Limitations and idiosyncrasies due to the action of the Ego in previous earth-lives, be it remembered.

due to no blind chance, to no innate qualities through hereditary tendencies—though that which is known as atavism may often intensify these faculties—but to an accumulation of individual antecedent experiences of the Ego in its preceding life and lives. For, omniscient in its essence and nature, it still requires experience, through its *personalities*, of the things of earth, earthly on the objective plane, in order to apply the fruition of that abstract experience to them. And, adds our philosophy, the cultivation of certain aptitudes throughout a long series of past incarnations must finally culminate, in some one life, in a blooming forth as *genius*, in one or another direction" (*Lucifer* for November, 1889, pp. 229-230). For the manifestation of true genius, purity of life is an essential condition.

Kâma-Manas is the personal self of man; we have already seen that the quaternary, as a whole, is the personality, "the shadow," and the lower Manas gives the individualizing touch that makes the personality recognize itself as "I". It becomes intellectual, it recognizes itself as separate from all other selves; deluded by the separateness it *feels*, it does not realize a unity beyond all that it is able to sense. And the lower Manas, attracted by the vividness of the material life-impressions, swayed by the rush of the kâmic emotions, passions and desires, attracted to all material things, blinded and deafened by the storm-voices among which it is plunged —the lower Manas is apt to forget the pure and serene glory of its birthplace, and to throw itself into the turbulence which gives rapture in lieu of peace. And be it remembered, it is this very lower Manas that yields the last touch of delight to the senses and to the animal nature; for what is passion that can neither anticipate nor remember, where is ecstasy without the subtle force of imagination, the delicate colours of fancy and of dream?

But there may be chains yet more strong and constraining, binding the lower Manas fast to earth. They are forged of ambition, of desire for fame, be it for that of the statesman's power, or of supreme intellectual achievement. So long as any work is wrought for sake of love, or praise, or even recognition that the work is "mine" and not another's; so long as in the heart's remotest chambers one subtlest yearning remains to be recognized as separate from all; so long, however grand the ambition, however far-reaching the charity, however lofty the achievement, Manas is tainted with Kâma, and is not pure as its source.

Manas in Activity.

We have already seen that the fifth principle is dual in its aspect during each period of earth-life, and that the lower Manas united to Kâma, spoken of conveniently as Kâma-Manas, functions in the brain and nervous system of man. We need to carry our investigation a little further in order to distinguish clearly between the activity of the higher and of the lower Manas, so that the working of the mind in man may become less obscure to us than it is at present to many.

Now the cells of the brain and nervous system (like all other cells) are composed of minute particles of matter, called molecules (literally, little heaps). These molecules do not touch each other, but are held grouped together by that manifestation of the Eternal Life which we call attraction. Not being in contact with each other they are able to vibrate to and fro if set in motion, and, as a matter of fact, they are in a state of continual vibration. H. P. Blavatsky points out (*Lucifer*, October, 1890, pp. 92, 93) that molecular motion is the lowest and most material form of the One Eternal Life, itself motion as the "Great Breath," and the source of all motion on every plane of the universe. In the Sanskrit, the roots of the terms for spirit, breath, being and motion are essentially the same, and Râma Prasâd says that "all these roots have for their origin the sound produced by the breath of animals"—the sound of expiration and inspiration.

Now the lower mind, or Kâma-Manas, acts on the molecules of the nervous cells by motion, and sets them vibrating, so starting mind-consciousness on the physical plane. Manas itself could not affect these molecules; but its ray, the lower Manas, having clothed itself in astral matter and united itself to the kâmic elements, is able to set the physical molecules in motion, and so give rise to "brain-consciousness," including the brain-memory and all the other functions of the human mind, as we know it in its ordinary activity. These manifestations, "like all other phenomena on the material plane . . . *must* be related in their final analysis to the world of vibration," says H. P. Blavatsky. But, she goes on to point out, "in their origin they belong to a different and a higher world of harmony". Their origin is in the manasic essence, in the ray; but on the material plane, acting on the molecules of the brain, they are translated into vibrations.

This action of the Kâma-Manas is spoken of by Theosophists as *psychic*. All mental and passional activities are due to this psychic energy, and its manifestations are necessarily conditioned by the physical apparatus through which it acts. We have already seen this broadly stated (*ante*, pp. 29, 30), and the *rationale* of the statement will now be apparent. If the molecular constitution of the brain be fine, and if the working of the specifically kâmic organs (liver, spleen, etc.) be healthy and pure—so as not to injure the molecular constitution of the nerves which put them into communication with the brain—then the psychic breath, as it sweeps through the instrument, awakens in this true Æolian harp harmonious and exquisite melodies; whereas if the molecular constitution be gross or poor, if it be disordered by the emanations of alcohol, if the blood be poisoned by gross living or sexual excesses, the strings of the Æolian harp become too loose or too tense, clogged with dirt or frayed with harsh usage, and when the psychic breath passes over them they remain dumb or give out harsh discordant notes, not because the breath is absent, but because the strings are in evil case.

It will now, I think, be clearly understood that what we call mind, or intellect, is, in H. P. Blavatsky's words, "a pale and too often distorted reflection" of Manas itself, or our fifth principle; Kâma-Manas is "the rational, but earthly or physical intellect of man, incased in, and bound by, matter, therefore subject to the influence of the latter"; it is the "lower self, or that which manifesting through our *organic* system, acting on this plane of illusion, imagines itself the *Ego sum*, and thus falls into what Buddhist philosophy brands as the 'heresy of separateness'". It is the human personality, from which proceeds "the psychic, *i.e.*, 'terrestrial wisdom' at best, as it is influenced by all the chaotic stimuli of the human or rather animal passions of the living body" (*Lucifer*, October, 1890, p. 179).

A clear understanding of the fact that Kâma-Manas belongs to the human personality, that it functions in and through the physical brain, that it acts on the molecules of the brain, setting them into vibration, will very much facilitate the comprehension by the student of the doctrine of reincarnation. That great subject will be dealt with in another volume of this series, and I do not propose to dwell upon it here, more than to remind the student to take careful note of the fact that the lower Manas is a ray from the immortal Thinker, *illuminating a personality*, and that all the functions which are brought into activity in the brain-consciousness are functions correlated to the particular brain, to the particular personality, in which they occur. The brain-molecules that are set vibrating are material organs in the man of flesh; they did not exist as brain-molecules before his conception, nor do they persist as brain-molecules after his disintegration. Their functional activity is limited by the limits of his personal life, the life of the body, the life of the transient personality.

Now the faculty of which we speak as memory on the physical plane depends on the response of these very brain-molecules to the impulse of the lower Manas, and there is no link between the brains of successive personalities except through the higher Manas, that sends out its ray to inform and enlighten them successively. It follows, then, inevitably, that unless the consciousness of man can rise from the physical and kâma-manasic planes to the plane of the higher Manas, no memory of one personality can reach over to another. The memory of the personality belongs to the transitory part of man's complex nature, and those only can recover the memory of their past lives who can raise their consciousness to the plane of the immortal Thinker, and can, so to speak, travel in consciousness up and down the ray which is the bridge between the personal man that perishes and the immortal man that endures. If, while we are cased in the man of flesh, we can raise our consciousness along the ray that connects our lower with our true Self, and so reach the higher Manas, we find there stored in the memory of that eternal Ego the whole records of our past lives on earth, and we can bring back those records to our brain-memory by way of that same ray, through which we can climb upwards to our "Father". But this is an achievement that belongs to a late stage of human evolution, and until this is reached the successive personalities informed by the manasic rays are separated from each other, and no memory bridges over the gulf between. The fact is obvious enough to any one who thinks the matter out, but as the difference between the personality and the immortal individuality is somewhat unfamiliar in the West, it may be well to remove a possible stumbling-block from the student's path.

Now the lower Manas may do one of three things: It may rise towards its source, and by unremitting and strenuous efforts become one with its "Father in heaven," or the higher Manas—Manas uncontaminated with earthly elements, unsoiled and pure. Or it may partially aspire and partially tend downwards, as indeed is mostly the case with the average man. Or, saddest fate of all, it may become so clogged with the kâmic elements as to become one with them, and be finally wrenched away from its parent and perish.

Before considering these three fates, there are a few more words to be said touching the activity of the lower Manas.

As the lower Manas frees itself from Kâma, it becomes the sovereign of the lower part of man, and manifests more and more of its true and essential nature.

In Kâma is desire, moved by bodily needs, and will, which is the outgoing energy of the Self in Manas, is often led captive by the turbulent physical impulses. But the lower Manas, "whenever it disconnects itself, for the time being, from Kâma, becomes the guide of the highest mental faculties, and is the organ of the free-will in physical man" (*Lucifer*, October, 1890, p. 94). But the condition of this freedom is that Kâma shall be subdued, shall lie prostrate beneath the feet of the conqueror; if the maiden Will is to be set free, the manasic St. George must slay the kâmic dragon that holds her captive; for while Kâma is unconquered, Desire will be master of Will.

Again, as the lower Manas frees itself from Kâma, it becomes more and more capable of transmitting to the human personality with which it is connected the impulses that reach it from its source. It is then, as we have seen, that genius flashes forth, the light from the higher Ego streaming through the lower Manas to the brain, and manifesting itself to the world. So also, as H. P. Blavatsky points out, such action may raise a man above the normal level of human power. "The higher Ego," she says, "cannot act directly on the body, as its consciousness belongs to quite another plane and planes of ideation; the lower self does; and its action and behaviour depend on its free-will and choice as to whether it will gravitate more towards its parent ('the Father in heaven') or the 'animal' which it informs, the man of flesh. The higher Ego, as part of the essence of the Universal Mind, is unconditionally omniscient on its own plane, and only potentially so in our terrestrial sphere, as it has to act solely through its *alter ego* the personal self. Now . . . the former is the vehicle of all knowledge of the past, the present and the future, and . . . it is from this fountain-head that its 'double' catches occasional glimpses of that which is beyond the senses of man, and transmits them to certain brain-cells (unknown to science in their functions), thus making of man a *seer*, a soothsayer and a prophet" (*Lucifer*, November, 1890, p. 179). This is the real seership, and on it a few words must be said presently. It is, naturally, extremely rare, and precious as it is rare. A "faint and distorted reflection" of it is found in what is called mediumship, and of this H. P. Blavatsky says: "Now what is a medium? The term medium, when not applied to things and objects, is supposed to be a person through whom the action of another person or being is either manifested or transmitted. Spiritualists, believing in communications with disembodied spirits, and that these can manifest through, or impress sensitives to transmit messages from them, regard mediumship as a blessing and a great privilege. We Theosophists, on the other hand, who do not believe in the 'communion of spirits' as Spiritualists do, regard the gift as one of the most dangerous of abnormal nervous diseases. A medium is simply one in whose personal Ego, or terrestrial mind, the percentage of astral light so preponderates as to impregnate with it his whole physical constitution. Every organ and cell thereby is attuned, so to speak, and subject to an enormous and abnormal tension" (*Lucifer*, November, 1890, p. 183).

To return to the three fates spoken of above, any one of which may befall the lower Manas.

It may rise towards its source and become one with the Father in heaven. This triumph can only be gained by many successive incarnations, all consciously directed towards this end. As life succeeds life, the physical frame becomes more and more delicately attuned to vibrations responsive to the manasic impulses, so that gradually the manasic ray needs less and less of the coarser astral matter as its vehicle. "It is part of the mission of the manasic ray to get gradually rid of the blind deceptive element which, though it makes of it an actual spiritual entity on this plane, still brings it into so close contact with matter as to entirely becloud its divine nature and stultify its intuitions" (*Lucifer*, November, 1890, p. 182). Life after life it rids itself of this "blind deceptive element," until at last, master of Kâma, and with body responsive to mind, the ray becomes one with its radiant source, the lower nature is wholly attuned to the higher, and the Adept stands forth complete, the "Father and the Son" having become one on all planes, as they have been always "one in heaven". For him the wheel of incarnation is over, the cycle of necessity is trodden. Henceforth he can incarnate at will, to do any special service to mankind; or he can dwell in the planes round earth without the physical body, helping in the further evolution of the globe and of the race.

It may partially aspire and partially tend downwards. This is the normal experience of the average man. All life is a battlefield, and the battle rages in the lower manasic region, where Manas wrestles with Kâma for empire over man. Anon aspiration conquers, the chains of sense are broken, and the lower Manas, with the radiance of its birth-place on it, soars upwards on strong wings, spurning the soil of earth. But, alas! too soon the pinions tire, they flag, they flutter, they cease to beat the air; and downwards falls the royal bird whose true realm is that of the higher air, and he flutters heavily to the bog of earth once more, and Kâma chains him down.

When the period of incarnation is over, and the gateway of death closes the road of earthly life, what becomes of the lower Manas in the case we are considering?

Soon after the death of the physical body Kàma-Manas is set free, and dwells for a while on the astral plane clothed with a body of astral matter. From this all of the manasic ray that is pure and unsoiled gradually disentangles itself, and, after a lengthy period spent on the lower levels of Devachan, it returns to its source, carrying with it such of its life experiences as are of a nature fit for assimilation with the higher Ego. Manas thus again becomes one during the latter part of the period which intervenes between two incarnations. The manasic Ego, brooded over by Âtmâ-Buddhi—the two highest principles in the human constitution, not yet considered by us—passes into the devachanic state of consciousness, resting from the weariness of the life-struggle through which it has passed. The experiences of the earth-life just closed are carried into the manasic consciousness by the lower ray withdrawn into its source. They make the devachanic state a continuation of earth-life, shorn of its sorrows, a completion of the wishes and desires of earth-life, so far as those were pure and noble. The poetic phrase that "the mind creates its own heaven" is truer than many may have imagined, for everywhere man *is* what he *thinks*, and in the devachanic state the mind is unfettered by the gross physical matter through which it works on the objective plane. The devachanic period is the time for the assimilation of life experiences, the regaining of equilibrium, ere a new journey is commenced. It is the day that succeeds the night of earth-life, the alternative of the objective manifestation. Periodicity is here, as everywhere else in nature, ebb and flow, throb and rest, the rhythm of the Universal Life. This devachanic state of consciousness lasts for a period of varying length, proportioned to the stage reached in evolution, the Devachan of the average man being said to extend over some fifteen hundred years.

Meanwhile, that portion of the impure garment of the lower Manas which remains entangled with Kâma gives to the desire-body a somewhat confused consciousness, a broken memory of the events of the life just closed. If the emotions and passions were strong and the manasic element weak during the period of incarnation, the desire-body will be strongly energized, and will persist in its activity for a considerable length of time after the death of the physical body. It will also show a considerable amount of consciousness, as much of the manasic ray will have been overpowered by the vigorous kâmic elements, and will have remained entangled in them. If, on the other hand, the earth-life just closed was characterized by mentality and purity rather than by passion, the desire-body, being but poorly energized, will be a pale simulacrum of the person to whom it belonged, and will fade away, disintegrate and perish before any long period has elapsed.

The "spook" already mentioned (*ante*, pp. 20, 21) will now be understood. It may show very considerable intelligence, if the manasic element be still largely present, and this will be the case with the desire-body of persons of strong animal nature and forcible though coarse intellect. For intelligence working in a very powerful kâmic personality will be exceedingly strong and energetic, though not subtle or delicate, and the spook of such a person, still further vitalized by the magnetic currents of persons yet living in the body, may show much intellectual ability of a low type. But such a spook is conscienceless, devoid of good impulses, tending towards disintegration, and communications with it can work for evil only, whether we regard them as prolonging its vitality by the currents which it sucks up from the bodies and kâmic elements of the living, or as exhausting the vitality of these living persons and polluting them with astral connections of an altogether undesirable kind.

Nor should it be forgotten that, without attending séance-rooms at all, living persons may come into objectionable contact with these kâmic spooks. As already mentioned, they are attracted to places in which the animal part of man is chiefly catered for; drinking-houses, gambling saloons, brothels—all these places are full of the vilest magnetism, are very whirlpools of magnetic currents of the foulest type. These attract the spooks magnetically, and they drift to such psychic maëlstroms of all that is earthly and sensual. Vivified by currents so congenial to their own, the desire-bodies become more active and potent; impregnated with the emanations of passions and desires which they can no longer physically satisfy, their magnetic currents reinforce the similar currents in the live persons, action and reaction continually going on, and the animal natures of the living become more potent and less controlled by the will as they are played on by these forces of the kâmic world. Kâma-loka (from *loka*, a place, and so the place for Kâma) is a name often used to designate that plane of the astral world to which these spooks belong, and from this ray forth magnetic currents of poisonous character, as from a pest-house float out germs of disease which may take root and grow in the congenial soil of some poorly vitalized physical body.

It is very possible that many will say, on reading these statements, that Theosophy is a revival of mediæval superstitions and will lead to imaginary terrors. Theosophy explains mediæval superstitions, and shows the natural facts on which they were founded and from which they drew their vitality. If there are planes in nature other than the physical, no amount of reasoning will get rid of them and belief in their existence will constantly reappear; but knowledge will give them their intelligible place in the universal order, and will prevent superstition by an accurate understanding of their nature, and of the laws under which they function. And let it be remembered that persons whose consciousness is normally on the physical plane can protect themselves from undesirable influences by keeping their minds clean and their wills strong. We protect ourselves best against disease by maintaining our bodies in vigorous health; we cannot guard ourselves against invisible germs, but we can prevent our bodies from becoming suitable soil for the growth and development of the germs. Nor need we deliberately throw ourselves in the way of infection. So also as regards these malign germs from the astral plane. We can prevent the formation of kâma-manasic soil in which they can germinate and develop, and we need not go into evil places, nor deliberately encourage receptivity and mediumistic tendencies. A strong active will and a pure heart are our best protection.

There remains the third possibility for Kâma-Manas, to which we must now turn our attention, the fate spoken of earlier as "terrible in its consequences, which may befall the kâmic principle".

It may break away from its source, made one with Kâma instead of with the higher Manas. This is, fortunately, a rare event, as rare at one pole of human life as the complete re-union with the higher Manas is rare at the other. But still the possibility remains and must be stated.

The personality may be so strongly controlled by Kâma that, in the struggle between the kâmic and manasic elements, the victory may remain wholly with the former. The lower Manas may become so enslaved that its essence may be frayed thinner and thinner by the constant rub and strain, until at last persistent yielding to the promptings of desire bears its inevitable fruit, and the slender link which unites the higher to the lower Manas, the "silver thread that binds it to the Master," snaps in two. Then, during earth-life, the lower quaternary is wrenched away from the Triad to which it was linked, and the higher nature is severed wholly from the lower. The human being is rent in twain, the brute has broken itself free, and it goes forth unbridled, carrying with it the reflections of that manasic light which should have been its guide through the desert of life. A more dangerous brute it is than its fellows of the unevolved animal world, just because of these fragments in it of the higher mentality of man. Such a being, human in form but brute in nature, human in appearance but without human ruth, or love, or justice—such a one may now and then be met with in the haunts of men, putrescent while still living, a thing to shudder at with deepest, if hopeless, compassion. What is its fate after the funeral knell has tolled?

Ultimately, there is the perishing of the personality that has thus broken away from the principles that can alone give it immortality. But a period of persistence lies before it.

The desire-body of such a one is an entity of terrible potency, and it has this unique peculiarity, that it is able under certain rare conditions to reincarnate in the world of men. It is not a mere "spook" on the way to disintegration; it has retained, entangled in its coils, too much of the manasic element to permit of such natural dissipation in space. It is sufficiently an independent entity, lurid instead of radiant, with manasic flame rendered foul instead of purifying, as to be able to take to itself garment of flesh once more and dwell as man with men. Such a man—if the word may be indeed applied to the mere human shell with brute interior—passes through a period of earth-life the natural foe of all who are still normal in their humanity. With no instincts save those of the animal, driven only by passion, never even by emotion, with a cunning that no brute can rival, a deliberate wickedness that plans evil in fashion unknown to the mere frankly natural impulses of the animal world, the reincarnated entity touches ideal vileness. Such soil the page of human history as the monsters of iniquity that startle us now and again into a wondering cry, "Is this a human being?" Sinking lower with each successive incarnation, the evil force gradually wears itself out, and such a personality perishes, separated from the source of life. It finally disintegrates, to be worked up into other forms of living things, but as a separate existence it is lost. It is a bead broken off the thread of life, and the immortal Ego that incarnated in that personality has lost the experience of that incarnation, has reaped no harvest from that life-sowing. Its ray has brought nothing back, its life-work for that birth has been a total and complete failure, whereof nothing remains to weave into the fabric of its own eternal Self.

Subtle Forms of the Fourth and Fifth Principles.

The student will already have fully realized that "an astral body" is a loose term that may cover a variety of different forms. It may be well at this stage to sum up the subtle types sometimes inaccurately called astral that belong to the fourth and fifth principles.

During life a true astral body may be projected—formed, as its name implies, of astral matter—but, unlike the etheric double, dowered with intelligence, and able to travel to a considerable distance from the physical body to which it belongs. This is the desire-body, and it is, as we have seen, a vehicle of consciousness. It is projected by mediums and sensitives unconsciously, and by trained students consciously. It can travel with the speed of thought to a distant place, can there gather impressions from surrounding objects, can bring back those impressions to the physical body. In the case of a medium it can convey them to others by means of the physical body still entranced, but as a rule when the sensitive comes out of trance, the brain does not retain the impressions thus made upon it, and no trace is left in the memory of the experiences thus acquired. Sometimes, but this is rare, the desire-body is able sufficiently to affect the brain by the vibrations it sets up, to leave a lasting impression thereon, and then the sensitive is able to recall the knowledge acquired during trance. The student learns to impress on his brain the knowledge gained in the desire-body, his will being active while that of the medium is passive.

This desire-body is the agent unconsciously used by clairvoyants when their vision is not merely the seeing in the astral light. This astral form does then really travel to distant places, and may appear there to persons who are sensitive or who chance for the time to be in an abnormal nervous condition. Sometimes it appears to them—when very faintly informed by consciousness—as a vaguely outlined form, not noticing its surroundings. Such a body has appeared near the time of death at places distant from the dying person, to those who were closely united to the dying by ties of blood, of affection, or of hatred. More highly energized, it will show intelligence and emotion, as in some cases on record, in which dying mothers have visited their children residing at a distance, and have spoken in their last moments of what they had seen and done. The desire-body is also set free in many cases of disease—as is the etheric double—as well as in sleep and in trance. Inactivity of the physical body is a condition of such astral voyagings.

The desire-body seems also occasionally to appear in séance-rooms, giving rise to some of the more intellectual phenomena that take place. It must not be confounded with the "spook," already sufficiently familiar to the reader, the latter being always the kâmic or kâma-manasic remains of a dead person, whereas the body we are now dealing with is the projection of an astral double from a living person.

A higher form of subtle body, belonging to Manas, is that known as the Mâyâvi Rûpa, or "body of illusion". The Mâyâvi Rûpa is a subtle body formed by the consciously directed will of the Adept or disciple; it may, or may not, resemble the physical body, the form given to it being suitable to the purpose for which it is projected. In this body the full consciousness dwells, for it is merely the mental body rearranged. The Adept or disciple can thus travel at will, without the burden of the physical body, in the full exercise of every faculty, in perfect self-consciousness. He makes the Mâyâvi Rûpa visible or invisible at will—on the physical plane—and the phrase often used by chelâs and others as to seeing an Adept "in his astral," means that he has visited them in his Mâyâvi Rûpa. If he so choose, he can make it indistinguishable from a physical body, warm and firm to the touch as well as visible, able to carry on a conversation, at all points like a physical human being. But the power thus to form the true Mâyâvi Rûpa is confined to Adepts and chelâs; it cannot be done by the untrained student, however psychic he may naturally be, for it is a manasic and not a psychic creation, and it is only under the instruction of his Guru that the chelâ learns to form and use the "body of illusion".

The Higher Manas.

The immortal Thinker itself, as will by this time have become clear to the reader, can manifest itself but little on the physical plane at the present stage of human evolution. Yet we are able to catch some glimpses of the powers resident in it, the more as in the lower Manas we find those powers "cribbed, cabined and confined" indeed, but yet existing. Thus we have seen (p. 37) that the lower Manas "is the organ of the freewill in physical man". Freewill resides in Manas itself, in Manas the representative of Mahat, the Universal Mind. From Manas comes the feeling of liberty, the knowledge that we can rule ourselves—really the knowledge that the higher nature in us can rule the lower, let that lower nature rebel and struggle as it may. Once let our consciousness identify itself with Manas instead of with Kâma, and the lower nature becomes the animal we bestride, it is no longer the "I". All its plungings, its struggles, its fights for mastery, are then outside us, not within us, and we rein it in and hold it as we rein in a plunging steed and subdue it to our will.

On this question of freewill I venture to quote from an article of my own that appeared in the *Path* :—

"Unconditioned will alone can be absolutely free: the unconditioned and the absolute are one: all that is conditioned must, by virtue of that conditioning, be relative and therefore partially bound. As that will evolves the universe, it becomes conditioned by the laws of its own manifestation. The manasic entities are differentiations of that will, each conditioned by the nature of its manifesting potency, but, while conditioned without, it is free within its own sphere of activity, so being the image in its own world of the universal will in the universe. Now as this will, acting on each successive plane, crystallizes itself more and more densely as matter, the manifestation is conditioned by the material in which it works, while, relatively to the material, it is itself free. So at each stage the inner freedom appears in consciousness, while yet investigation shows that that freedom works within the limits of the plane of manifestation on which it is acting, free to work upon the lower, yet hindered as to manifestation by the unresponsiveness of the lower to its impulse. Thus the higher Manas, in whom resides freewill, so far as the lower quaternary is concerned—being the offspring of Mahat, the third Logos, the Word, *i.e.*, the Will in manifestation—is limited in its manifestation in our lower nature by the sluggishness of the response of the personality to its impulses; in the lower Manas itself—as immersed in that personality—resides the will with which we are familiar, swayed by passions, by appetites, by desires, by impressions coming from without, yet able to assert itself among them all, by virtue of its essential nature, one with that higher Ego of which it is the ray. It is free, as regards all below it, able to act on Kâma and on the physical body, however much its full expression may be thwarted and hindered by the crudeness of the material in which it is working. Were the will the mere outcome of the physical body, of the desires and passions, whence could arise the sense of the 'I' that can judge, can desire, can overcome? It acts from a higher plane, is royal as touching the lower whenever it claims the royalty of birthright, and the very struggle of its self-assertion is the best testimony to the fact that in its nature it is free. And so, passing to lower planes, we find in each grade this freedom of the higher as ruling the lower, yet, on the plane of the lower, hindered in manifestation. Reversing the process and starting from the lower, the same truth becomes manifest. Let a man's limbs be loaded with fetters, and crude material iron will prevent the manifestation of the muscular and nervous force with which they are instinct: none the less is that force present, though hindered for the moment in its activity. Its strength may be shown in its very efforts to break the chains that bind it: there is no power in the iron to prevent the free giving out of the muscular energy, though the phenomena of motion may be hindered. But while this energy cannot be ruled by the physical nature below it, its expenditure is determined by the kâmic principle; passions and desires can set it going, can direct and control it. The muscular and nervous energy cannot rule the passions and desires, they are free as regards it, it is determined by their interposition. Yet again Kâma may be ruled, controlled, determined by the will; as touching the manasic principle it is bound, not free, and hence the sense of freedom in choosing which desire shall be gratified, which act performed. As the lower Manas rules Kâma, the lower quaternary takes its rightful position of subserviency to the higher triad, and is determined by a will it recognizes as above itself, and, as regards itself, a will that is free. Here in many a mind will spring the question, 'And what of the will of the higher Manas; is that in turn determined by what is above it, while it is free to all below?' But we have reached a point where the intellect fails us, and where language may not easily utter that which the Spirit senses in those higher realms. Dimly only can we feel that there, as everywhere else, the truest freedom must be in harmony with law, and that voluntary acceptance of the function of acting as channel of the universal will must unite into one perfect liberty and perfect obedience."

This is truly an obscure and difficult problem, but the student will find much light fall on it by following the lines of thought thus traced.

Another power resident in the higher Manas and manifested on the lower planes by those in whom the higher Manas is consciously master, is that of creation of forms by the will. The *Secret Doctrine* says: "Kriyâshakti. The mysterious power of thought which enables it to produce external, perceptible, phenomenal results by its own inherent energy. The ancients held that *any idea will manifest itself externally if one's attention is deeply concentrated upon it.* Similarly an *intense volition will be followed by the desired results*" (vol. i., p. 312). Here is the secret of all true "magic," and as the subject is an important one, and as Western science is beginning to touch its fringe, a separate section is devoted to its consideration farther on, in order not to break the connected outline here given of the principles.

Again, we have learned from H. P. Blavatsky that Manas, or the higher Ego, as "part of the essence of the Universal Mind, is unconditionally omniscient on its own plane," when it has fully developed self-consciousness by its evolutionary experiences, and "is the vehicle of all knowledge of the past and present, and the future". When this immortal entity is able through its ray, the lower Manas, to impress the brain of a man, that man is one who manifests abnormal qualities, is a genius or a seer. The conditions of seership are thus laid down :—

"The former [the visions of the true seer] can be obtained by one of two means : (*a*) on the condition of paralyzing at will the *memory* and the instinctual independent action of all the material organs and even cells in the body of flesh, an act which, when once the light of the higher Ego has consumed and subjected for ever the passional nature of the personal lower Ego, is easy, but requires an adept ; and (*b*) of being a reincarnation of one who, in a previous birth, had attained through extreme purity of life and efforts in the right direction almost to a Yogi-state of holiness and saintship. There is also a third possibility of reaching in mystic visions the plane of the higher Manas ; but it is only occasional, and does not depend on the will of the seer, but on the extreme weakness and exhaustion of the material body through illness and suffering. The Seeress of Prevorst was an instance of the latter case ; and Jacob Boehme of our second category" (*Lucifer*, November, 1890, p. 183).

The reader will now be in a position to grasp the difference between the workings of the higher Ego and of its ray. Genius, which *sees* instead of arguing, is of the higher Ego; true intuition is one of its faculties. Reason, the weighing and balancing quality which arranges the facts gathered by observation, balances them one against the other, argues from them, draws conclusions from them—this is the exercise of the lower Manas through the brain apparatus; its instrument is ratiocination; by induction it ascends from the known to the unknown, building up a hypothesis: by deduction it descends again to the known, verifying its hypothesis by fresh experiment.

Intuition, as we see by its derivation, is simply insight—a process as direct and swift as bodily vision. It is the exercise of the eyes of the intelligence, the unerring recognition of a truth presented on the mental plane. It sees with certainty, its vision is unclouded, its report unfaltering. No proof can add to the certitude of its recognition, for it is beyond and above the reason. Often our instincts, blinded and confused by passions and desires, are miscalled intuitions, and a mere kâmic impulse is accepted as the sublime voice of the higher Manas. Careful and prolonged self-training is necessary ere that voice can be recognized with certainty, but of one thing we may feel very sure: so long as we are in the vortex of the personality, so long as the storms of desires and appetites howl around us, so long as the waves of emotion toss us to and fro, so long the voice of the higher Manas cannot reach our ears. Not in the fire or the whirlwind, not in the thunderclap or the storm, comes the mandate of the higher Ego: only when there has fallen the stillness of a silence that can be felt, only when the very air is motionless and the calm is profound, only when the man wraps his face in a mantle which closes his ears even to the silence that is of earth, then only sounds the voice that is stiller than the silence, the voice of his true Self.

On this H. P. Blavatsky has written in *Isis Unveiled*: "Allied to the physical half of man's nature is reason, which enables him to maintain his supremacy over the lower animals, and to subjugate nature to his uses. Allied to his spiritual part is his conscience, which will serve as his unerring guide through the besetment of the senses; for conscience is that instantaneous perception between right and wrong which can only be exercised by the spirit, which, being a portion of the divine wisdom and purity, is absolutely pure and wise. Its promptings are independent of reason, and it can only manifest itself clearly when unhampered by the baser attractions of our dual nature. Reason being a faculty of our physical brain, one which is justly defined as that of deducing inferences from premisses, and being wholly dependent on the evidence of other senses, cannot be a quality pertaining directly to our divine spirit. The latter *knqws* —hence all reasoning, which implies discussion and argument, would be useless. So an entity which, if it must be considered as a direct emanation from the eternal Spirit of Wisdom, has to be viewed as possessed of the same attributes as the essence or the whole of which it is part. Therefore it is with a certain degree of logic that the ancient Theurgists maintained that the rational part of man's soul (spirit) never entered wholly into the man's body, but only overshadowed him more or less through the irrational or astral soul, which serves as an intermediatory agent, or a medium between spirit and body. The man who has conquered matter sufficiently to receive the direct light from his shining *Augoeides*, feels truth intuitionally; he could not err in his judgment, notwithstanding all the sophisms suggested by cold reason, for he is *illuminated*. Hence, prophecy, vaticination, and the so-called divine inspiration, are simply the effects of this illumination from above by our own immortal spirit" (vol. i., pp. 305, 306).

This Augoeides, according to the belief of the Neo-Platonists, as according to the Theosophical teachings, "sheds more or less its radiance on the inner man, the astral soul" (*ibid*., p. 315), *i.e.*, in the now accepted terminology, on the kâma-manasic personality or lower Ego. (In reading *Isis Unveiled*, the student has to bear in mind the fact that when the book was written, the terminology was by no means even as fixed as it is now; in *Isis Unveiled* is the first modern attempt to translate into Western language the complicated Eastern ideas, and further experience has shown that many of the terms used to cover two or three conceptions may with advantage be restricted to one and thus rendered precise. Thus the "astral soul" must be understood in the sense given above.) Only as this lower Ego becomes pure from all breath of passion, as the lower Manas frees itself from Kâma, can the "shining one" impress it; H. P. Blavatsky tells us how initiates meet this higher Ego face to face. Having spoken of the trinity in man, Âtmâ-Buddhi-Manas, she goes on: "It is when this trinity, in anticipation of the final triumphant reunion beyond the gates of corporeal death, became for a few seconds a unity, that the candidate is allowed, at the moment of the initiation, to behold his future self. Thus we read in the Persian *Desatir* of the 'resplendent one'; in the Greek philosopher-initiates of the Augoeides—the self-shining 'blessed vision resident in the pure light'; in Porphyry, that Plotinus was united to his 'god' six times during his life-time, and so on" (*Isis Unveiled*, vol. ii., pp. 114, 115).

This trinity made into unity, again, is the "Christ" of all mystics. When, in the final initiation, the candidate has been outstretched on the floor or altarstone and has thus typified the crucifixion of the flesh, or lower nature, and when from this "death" he has "risen again" as the triumphant conqueror over sin and death, he then, in the supreme moment, sees before him the glorious presence and becomes "one with Christ," is himself the Christ. Thenceforth he may live in the body, but it has become his obedient instrument; he is united with his true Self, Manas made one with Âtmâ-Buddhi, and through the personality which he inhabits he wields his full powers as an immortal spiritual intelligence. While he was still struggling in the toils of the lower nature, Christ, the spiritual Ego, was daily crucified in him; but in the full Adept Christ has arisen triumphant, lord of himself and of nature. The long pilgrimage of Manas is over, the cycle of necessity is trodden, the wheel of rebirth ceases to turn, the Son of Man has been made perfect by suffering.

So long as this point has not been reached, "the Christ" is the object of aspiration. The ray is ever struggling to return to its source, the lower Manas ever aspiring to rebecome one with the higher. While this duality persists the continual yearning towards reunion felt by the noblest and purest natures is one of the most salient facts of the inner life, and it is this which clothes itself as prayer, as inspiration, as "seeking after God," as the longing for union with the divine. "My soul is athirst for God, for the living God," cries the eager Christian, and to tell him that this intense longing is a fancy and is futile is to make him turn aside from you as one who cannot understand, but whose insensibility does not alter the fact. The Occultist recognizes in this cry the inextinguishable impulse upwards of the lower Self to the higher from which it is separated, but the attraction of which it vividly feels. Whether the person pray to the Buddha, to Vishnu, to Christ, to the Virgin, to the Father, it matters not at all; these are questions of mere dialect, not of essential fact. In all the Manas united to Âtmâ-Buddhi is the real object, veiled under what name the changing time or race may give; at once the ideal humanity and the "personal God," the "God-Man" found in all religions, "God incarnate," the "Word made flesh," the Christ who must "be born in" each, with whom the believer must be made one.

And this leads us on to the last planes with which we are concerned, the planes of Spirit, using that much abused word merely as the opposite pole to matter; here only very general ideas can be grasped by us, but it is necessary none the less to try to grasp these ideas if we are to complete, however poorly, our conception of man.

PRINCIPLES VI. AND VII. ÂTMÂ-BUDDHI, THE "SPIRIT".

As the completion of the thought of the last section, we will look at Atmâ-Buddhi first in its connection with Manas, and will then proceed to a somewhat more general view of it as the "Monad". The clearest and best description of the human trinity, Atmâ-Buddhi-Manas, will be found in the *Key to Theosophy*, in which H. P. Blavatsky gives the following definitions:—

"The HIGHER SELF is	*Âtmâ*, the inseparable ray of the Universal and ONE SELF. It is the God *above*, more than within us. Happy the man who succeeds in saturating his *inner Ego* with it.
"The SPIRITUAL *divine* EGO is	the spiritual soul, or *Buddhi*, in close union with *Manas*, the mind-principle, without which it is no EGO at all, but only the Âtmic vehicle.
"The INNER or HIGHER EGO is	*Manas*, the fifth principle, so called, independently of Buddhi. The mind-principle is only the Spiritual Ego when merged into one with Buddhi. . . . It is the permanent individuality or the reincarnating Ego" (pp. 175, 176).

Âtmâ must then be regarded as the most abstract part of man's nature, the "breath" which needs a body for its manifestation. It is the one reality, that which manifests on all planes, the essence of which all our principles are but aspects. The one Eternal Existence, wherefrom are all things, which embodies one of its aspects in the universe, that which we speak of as the One Life—this Eternal Existence rays forth as Âtmâ, the very Self alike of the universe and of man; their innermost core, their very heart, that in which all things inhere. In itself incapable of direct manifestation on lower planes, yet That without which no lower planes could come into existence, it clothes itself in Buddhi, as its vehicle, or medium of further manifestation. "Buddhi is the faculty of cognizing, the channel through which divine knowledge reaches the Ego, the discernment of good and evil, also divine conscience, and the spiritual Soul, which is the vehicle of Âtmâ" (*Secret Doctrine*, vol. i., p. 3). It is often spoken of as the principle of spiritual discernment. But Âtmâ-Buddhi, a universal principle, needs individualizing ere experience can be gathered and self-consciousness attained. So the mind-principle is united to Âtmâ-Buddhi, and the human trinity is complete. Manas becomes the *spiritual* Ego only when merged in Buddhi; Buddhi becomes the spiritual *Ego* only when united to Manas; in the union of the two lies the evolution of the Spirit, self-conscious on all planes. Hence Manas strives upward to Âtmâ-Buddhi, as the lower Manas strives upward to the higher, and hence, in relation to the higher Manas, Âtmâ-Buddhi, or Âtmâ, is often spoken of as "the Father in Heaven," as the higher Manas is itself thus described in relation to the lower (see *ante*, p. 40). The lower Manas gathers experience to carry it back to its source; the higher Manas accumulates the store throughout the cycle of reincarnation; Buddhi becomes assimilated with the higher Manas; and these, permeated with the Atmic light, one with that True Self, the trinity becomes a unity, the Spirit is self-conscious on all planes, and the object of the manifested universe is attained.

But no words of mine can avail to explain or to describe that which is beyond explanation and beyond description. Words can but blunder along on such a theme, dwarfing and distorting it. Only by long and patient meditation can the student hope vaguely to sense something greater than himself, yet something which stirs at the innermost core of his being. As to the steady gaze directed at the pale evening sky, there appears after awhile, faintly and far away, the soft glimmer of a star, so to the patient gaze of the inner vision there may come the tender beam of the spiritual star, if but as a mere suggestion of a far-off world. Only to a patient and persevering purity will that light arise, and blessed beyond all earthly blessedness is he who sees but the palest shimmer of that transcendent radiance.

With such ideas as to "Spirit," the horror with which Theosophists shrink from ascribing the trivial phenomena of the séance-room to "spirits" will be readily understood. Playing on musical-boxes, talking through trumpets, tapping people on the head, carrying accordions round the room—these things may be all very well for astrals, spooks, and elementals, but who can assign them to "spirits," who has any conception of Spirit worthy of the name? Such vulgarization and degradation of the most sublime conceptions as yet evolved by man are surely subjects for the keenest regret, and it may well be hoped that ere long these phenomena will be put in their true place, as evidence that the materialistic views of the universe are inadequate, instead of being exalted to a place they cannot fill as proofs of Spirit. No physical, no intellectual phenomena are proofs of the existence of Spirit. Only to the spirit can Spirit be demonstrated.

You cannot prove a proposition in Euclid to a dog; you cannot prove Âtmâ-Buddhi to Kâma and the lower Manas. As we climb, our view will widen, and when we stand on the summit of the Holy Mount the planes of Spirit shall lie before our opened vision.

The Monad in Evolution.

Perhaps a slightly more definite conception of Âtmâ-Buddhi may be obtained by the student, if he considers its work in evolution as the Monad. Now Âtmâ-Buddhi is identical with the universal Over-soul, "itself an aspect of the Unknown Root," the One Existence. When manifestation begins the Monad is "thrown downwards into matter," to propel forwards and force evolution (see *Secret Doctrine*, vol. ii., p. 115); it is the mainspring, so to speak, of all evolution, the impelling force at the root of all things. All the principles we have been studying are mere "variously differentiated aspects" of Âtmâ, the One Reality manifesting in our universe; it is in every atom, "the root of every atom individually and of every form collectively," and all the principles are fundamentally Âtmâ on different planes. The stages of its evolution are very clearly laid down in *Five Years of Theosophy*, pp. 273 *et seq.* There we are shown how it passes through the stages termed elemental, "nascent centres of forces," and reaches the mineral stage; from this it passes up through vegetable, animal, to man, vivifying every form. As we are taught in the *Secret Doctrine*: "The well-known Kabbalistic aphorism runs: 'A stone becomes a plant; a plant, a beast; the beast, a man; a man, a spirit; and the spirit, a god'. The 'spark' animates all the kingdoms in turn before it enters into and informs divine man, between whom and his predecessor, animal man, there is all the difference in the world. . . . The Monad . . . is, first of all, shot down by the law of evolution into the lowest form of matter—the mineral. After a sevenfold gyration incased in the stone, or that which will become mineral and stone in the Fourth Round, it creeps out of it, say as a lichen. Passing thence, through all the forms of vegetable matter, into what is termed animal matter, it has now reached the point in which it has become the germ, so to speak, of the animal, that will become the physical man" (vol. i., pp. 266, 267).

It is the Monad, Âtmâ-Buddhi, that thus vivifies every part and kingdom of nature, making all instinct with life and consciousness, one throbbing whole. "Occultism does not accept anything inorganic in the Kosmos. The expression employed by science, 'inorganic substance,' means simply that the latent life, slumbering in the molecules of so-called 'inert matter,' is incognizable. All is life and every atom of even mineral dust is a life, though beyond our comprehension and perception, because it is outside the range of the laws known to those who reject Occultism" (*Secret Doctrine*, vol. i., pp. 268, 269). And again: "Everything in the universe, throughout all its kingdoms, is conscious, *i.e.*, endowed with a consciousness of its own kind and on its own plane of perception. We men must remember that simply because *we* do not perceive any signs of consciousness which we can recognize, say in stones, we have no right to say that no consciousness exists there. There is no such thing as either 'dead' or 'blind' matter, as there is no 'blind' or 'unconscious' law" (p. 295).

How many of the great poets, with the sublime intuition of genius, have sensed this great truth! To them all nature pulses with life; they see life and love everywhere, in suns and planets as in the grains of dust, in rustling leaves and opening blossoms, in dancing gnats and gliding snakes. Each form manifests as much of the One Life as it is capable of expressing, and what is man that he should despise the more limited manifestations, when he compares himself as life-expression, not with the forms below him, but with the possibilities of expression that soar above him in infinite heights of being, which he can estimate still less than the stone can estimate him?

The student will readily see that we must regard this force at the centre of evolution as essentially *one*. There is but one Âtmâ-Buddhi in our universe, the universal Soul, everywhere present, immanent in all, the One Supreme Energy whereof all varying energies or forces are only differing forms. As the sunbeam is light or heat or electricity according to its conditioning environment, so is Âtmâ all-energy, differentiating on different planes. "As an abstraction, we will call it the One Life; as an objective and evident reality, we speak of a septenary scale of manifestation, which begins at the upper rung with the one unknowable causality, and ends as Omnipresent Mind and Life immanent in every atom of matter" (*Secret Doctrine*, vol. i., p. 163).

Its evolutionary course is very plainly outlined in a quotation given in the *Secret Doctrine*, and as students are very often puzzled over this unity of the Monad, I subjoin the statement. The subject is difficult, but it could not, I think, be more clearly put than it is in these sentences:—

"Now the monadic or cosmic essence (if such a term be permitted) in the mineral, vegetable, and animal, though the same throughout the series of cycles from the lowest elemental up to the Deva kingdom, yet differs in the scale of progression. It would be very misleading to imagine a Monad as a separate entity trailing its slow way in a distinct path through the lower kingdoms, and after an incalculable series of transformations flowering into a human being: in short, that the Monad of a Humboldt dates back to the Monad of an atom of hornblende. Instead of saying a 'Mineral Monad,' the more correct phraseology in physical science, which differentiates every atom, would of course have been to call it 'the Monad manifesting in that form of Prakriti called the mineral kingdom'. The atom, as represented in the ordinary scientific hypothesis, is not a particle of something, animated by a psychic something, destined after æons to blossom as a man. But it is a concrete manifestation of the universal energy which itself has not yet become individualized; a sequential manifestation of the one universal Monas. The ocean of matter does not divide into its potential and constituent drops until the sweep of the life-impulse reaches the stage of man-birth. The tendency towards segregation into individual Monads is gradual, and in the higher animals comes almost to the point. The Peripatetics applied the word Monas to the whole Kosmos in the pantheistic sense; and the Occultists, while accepting this thought for convenience' sake, distinguish the progressive stages of the evolution of the concrete from the abstract by terms of which the 'mineral, vegetable, animal, Monad,' etc., are examples. The term merely means that the tidal wave of spiritual evolution is passing through that arc of its circuit. The 'Monadic Essence' begins imperfectly to differentiate towards individual consciousness in the vegetable kingdom. As the Monads are uncompounded things, as correctly defined by Leibnitz, it is the spiritual essence which vivifies them in their degrees of differentiation, which properly constitutes the Monad—not the atomic aggregation, which is only the vehicle and the substance through which thrill the lower and the higher degrees of intelligence" (vol. i., p. 201).

The student who reads and weighs this passage will, at the cost of a little present trouble, save himself from much confusion in days to come. Let him first realize clearly that the Monad—"the spiritual essence" to which alone in strict accuracy the term Monad should be applied—is *one* all the universe over, that Âtmâ-Buddhi is not his, nor mine, nor the property of anybody in particular, but the spiritual essence energizing in all. So is electricity *one* all the world over; though it may be active in his machine or in mine, neither he nor I can call it distinctively our electricity. But—and here arises the confusion—when Âtmâ-Buddhi energizes in man, in whom Manas is active as an individualizing force, it is often spoken of as though the "atomic aggregation" were a separate Monad, and then we have "Monads," as in the above passage. This loose way of using the word will not lead to error if the student will remember that the individualizing process *is not on the spiritual plane*, but that Âtmâ-Buddhi *as seen through Manas* seems to share in the individuality of the latter. So if you hold pieces of variously coloured glass in your hand you may see through them a red sun, a blue sun, a yellow sun, and so on. None the less is there only the one sun shining down upon you, altered by the media through which you look at it. So we often meet the phrase "human Monads"; it should be "the Monad manifesting in the human kingdom"; but this somewhat pedantic accuracy would be likely only to puzzle a large number of people, and the looser popular phrase will not mislead when the principle of the unity on the spiritual plane is grasped, any more than we mislead by speaking of the rising of the sun. "The Spiritual Monad is one, universal, boundless, and impartite, whose rays, nevertheless, form what we, in our ignorance, call the 'individual Monads' of men" (*Secret Doctrine*, vol. i., p. 200).

Very beautifully and poetically is this unity in diversity put in one of the Occult Catechisms in which the Guru questions the Chela :—

"Lift thy head, O Lanoo ; dost thou see one or countless lights above thee, burning in the dark midnight sky ?"

"I sense one Flame, O Gurudeva ; I see countless undetached sparks burning in it."

"Thou sayest well. And now look around and into thyself. That light which burns inside thee, dost thou feel it different in any wise from the light that shines in thy brother-men ?"

"It is in no way different, though the prisoner is held in bondage by Karma, and though its outer garments delude the ignorant into saying, 'thy soul' and 'my soul'" (*Secret Doctrine*, vol. i., p. 145).

There ought not to be any serious difficulty now in grasping the stages of human evolution ; the Monad, which has been working its way as we have seen, reaches the point at which the human form can be built up on earth ; an etheric body and its physical counterpart are then developed, Prâna specialized from the great ocean of life, and Kâma evolved, all these principles, the lower quaternary, being brooded over by the Monad, energized by it, impelled by it, forced onward by it towards continually increasing perfection of form and capacity for manifesting the higher energies in Nature. This was animal, or physical man, evolved through two and a half

Races. But the Monad and the lower quaternary could not come into sufficiently close relation with each other; a link was yet wanting. "The Double Dragon [the Monad] has no hold upon the mere form. It is like the breeze where there is no tree or branch to receive and harbour it. It cannot affect the form where there is no agent of transmission, and the form knows it not" (*Secret Doctrine*, vol. ii., p. 60). Then, at the middle point just reached, in the middle, that is, of the Third Race, the lower Mânasaputra stepped in to inhabit the dwellings thus prepared for them, and to form the bridge between animal man and the Spirit, between the evolved quaternary and the brooding Âtmâ-Buddhi, to begin the long cycle of reincarnation which is to issue in the perfect man.

The "monadic inflow," or the evolution of the Monad from the animal into the human kingdom, continued through the Third Race on to the middle of the Fourth, the human population thus continually receiving fresh recruits, the birth of souls thus continuing through the second half of the Third Race and the first half of the Fourth. After this, the "central turning point" of the cycle of evolution, "no more Monads can enter the human kingdom. The door is closed for this cycle" (*Secret Doctrine*, vol. i., p. 205). Since then reincarnation has been the method of evolution, this individual reincarnation of the immortal Thinker in conjunction with Âtmâ-Buddhi replacing the collective indwelling of Âtmâ-Buddhi in lower forms of matter.

According to Theosophical teachings, humanity has now reached the Fifth Race, and we are in the fifth sub-race thereof, mankind on this globe in the present stage having before it the completion of the Fifth Race, and the rise, maturity and decay of the Sixth and Seventh

Races. But during all the ages necessary for this evolution there is no increase in the total number of reincarnating Egos; only a small proportion of these are reincarnated at any special time on our globe, so that the population may ebb and flow within very wide limits, and it will have been noticed that there is a rush of births after a local depopulation has been caused by exceptional mortality. There is room and to spare for all such fluctuations, having in view the difference between the total number of reincarnating Egos and the number actually incarnated at a given period.

Lines of Proof for an Untrained Inquirer.

It is natural and right that any thoughtful person, brought face to face with assertions such as those put forth in the preceding pages, should demand what proof is forthcoming to substantiate the propositions laid down. A reasonable person will not demand full and complete proof available to all comers, without study and without painstaking. He will admit that the advanced theories of a science cannot be demonstrated to one ignorant of its first principles, and he will be prepared to find that very much will have been alleged which can only be proved to those who have made some progress in their study. An essay on the higher mathematics, on the correlation of forces, on the atomic theory, on the molecular constitution of chemical compounds, would contain many statements the proofs of which would only be available for those who had devoted time and thought to the study of the elements of the science concerned; and so an unprejudiced person, confronted with the Theosophical view of the constitution of man, would readily admit that he could not expect complete demonstration until he had mastered the elements of Theosophical science.

None the less are there general proofs available in every science which suffice to justify its existence and to encourage study of its more recondite truths; and in Theosophy it is possible to indicate lines of proof which can be followed by the untrained inquirer, and which justify him in devoting time and pains to a study which gives promise of a wider and deeper knowledge of himself and of external nature than is otherwise attainable.

It is well to say at the outset that there is no proof available to the average inquirer of the existence of the three higher planes of which we have spoken. The realms of the Spirit and of the higher mind are closed to all save those who have evolved the faculties necessary for their investigation. Those who have evolved these faculties need no proof of the existence of those realms; to those who have not, no proof of their existence can be given. That there is *something* above the astral and the lower levels of the mental plane may indeed be proved by the flashes of genius, the lofty intuitions, that from time to time lighten the darkness of our lower world; but what that something is, only those can say whose inner eyes have been opened, who see where the race as a whole is still blind. But the lower planes are susceptible of proof, and fresh proofs are accumulating day by day. The Masters of Wisdom are using the investigators and thinkers of the Western world to make "discoveries" which tend to substantiate the outposts of the Theosophical position, and the lines which they are following are exactly those which are needed for the finding of natural laws which will justify the assertions of Theosophists with regard to the elementary "powers" and "phenomena" to which such exaggerated importance has been given. If it is found that we have undeniable facts which establish the existence of planes other than the physical on which consciousness can work; which establish the existence of senses and powers of perception other than those with which we are familiar in daily life; which establish the existence of powers of communication between intelligences without the use of mechanical apparatus, surely, under these circumstances, the Theosophist may claim that he has made out a *prima facie* case for further investigation of his doctrines.

Let us, then, confine ourselves to the lower planes of which we have spoken in the preceding pages, and the four lower principles in man which are correlated with these planes. Of these four we may dismiss one, that of Prâna, as none will challenge the fact of the existence of the energy we call "life"; the need of isolating it for purposes of study may be challenged, and in very truth the plane of Prâna, or the principle of Prâna, runs through all other planes, all other principles, interpenetrating all and binding all in one. There remain for our study the physical plane, the astral plane, the lower levels of the manasic plane. Can we substantiate these by proofs which will be accepted by those who are not yet Theosophists? I think we can.

First, as regards the physical plane. We need here to notice how the senses of man are correlated with the physical universe outside him, and how his knowledge of that universe is bounded by the power of his organs of sense to vibrate in response to vibrations set up outside him. He can hear when the air is thrown into vibrations into which the drum of his ear can also be thrown; if the vibration be so slow that the drum cannot vibrate in answer, the person does not hear any sound; if the vibration be so rapid that the drum cannot vibrate in answer, the person does not hear any sound. So true is this, that the limit of hearing in different persons varies with this power of vibration of the drums of their respective ears; one person is plunged in silence, while another is deafened by the keen shrilling that is throwing into tumult the air around both. The same principle holds good of sight; we see so long as the light waves are of a length to which our organs of sight can respond; below and beyond this length we are in darkness, let the ether vibrate as it may. The ant can see where we are blind, because its eye can receive and respond to etheric vibrations more rapid than we can sense.

All this suggests to any thoughtful person the idea that if our senses could be evolved to more responsiveness, new avenues of knowledge would be opened up even on the physical plane; this realized, it is not difficult to go a step farther, and to conceive that keener and subtler senses might exist which would open up, as it were, a new universe on a plane other than the physical.

Now this conception is true, and with the evolution of the astral senses the astral plane unfolds itself, and may be studied as really, as scientifically, as the physical universe can be. These astral senses exist in all men, but are latent in most, and generally need to be artificially forced, if they are to be used in the present stage of evolution. In a few persons they are normally present and become active without any artificial impulse. In very many persons they can be artificially awakened and developed. The condition, in all cases, of the activity of the astral senses is the passivity of the physical, and the more complete the passivity on the physical plane the greater the possibility of activity on the astral.

It is noteworthy that Western psychologists have found it necessary to investigate what is termed the "dream-consciousness," in order to understand the workings of consciousness as a whole. It is impossible to ignore the strange phenomena which characterize the workings of consciousness when it is removed from the limitations of the physical plane, and some of the most able and advanced of our psychologists do not think these workings to be in any way unworthy of the most careful and scientific investigation. All such workings are, in Theosophical language, on the astral plane, and the student who seeks for proof that there is an astral plane may here find enough and to spare. He will speedily discover that the laws under which consciousness works on the physical plane have no existence on the astral. *E.g.*, the laws of space and time, which are here the very conditions of thought, do not exist for consciousness when its activity is transferred to the astral world. Mozart hears a whole symphony as a single impression, "as in a fine and strong dream" (*Philosophy of Mysticism*, Du Prel, vol. i., p. 106), but has to work it out in successive details when he brings it back with him to the physical plane. The dream of a moment contains a mass of events that would take years to pass in succession in our world of space and time. The drowning man sees his life history in a few seconds. But it is needless to multiply instances.

The astral plane may be reached in sleep or in trance, natural or induced, *i.e.*, in any case in which the body is reduced to a condition of lethargy. It is in trance that it can best be studied, and here our inquirer will soon find proof that consciousness can work apart from the physical organism, unfettered by the laws that bind it while it works on the physical plane. Clairvoyance and clairaudience are among the most interesting of the phenomena that here lie open for investigation.

It is not necessary here to give a large number of cases of clairvoyance, for I am supposing that the inquirer intends to study for himself. But I may mention the case of Jane Rider, observed by Dr. Belden, her medical attendant, a girl who could read and write with her eyes carefully covered with wads of cotton wool, coming down to the middle of the cheek (*Isis Revelata*, vol. i., p. 37); of a clairvoyant observed by Schelling, who announced the death of a relative at a distance of 150 leagues, and stated that the letter containing the news of the death was on its way (*ibid.*, vol. ii., pp. 89-92); of Madame Lagandré, who diagnosed the internal state of her mother, giving a description that was proved to be correct by the post-mortem examination (*Somnolism and Psychism*, Dr. Haddock, pp. 54-56); of Emma, Dr. Haddock's somnambule, who constantly diagnosed diseases for him (*ibid.*, chap. vii.). Speaking generally, the clairvoyant can see and describe events which are taking place at a distance, or under circumstances that render physical sight impossible. *How is this done?* The facts are beyond dispute. They require explanation. We say that consciousness can work through senses other than the physical, senses unfettered by the limitations of space which exist for our bodily senses, and cannot by them be transcended. Those who deny the possibility of such working on what we call the astral plane should at least endeavour to present a hypothesis more reasonable than ours. Facts are stubborn things, and we have here a mass of facts proving the existence of conscious activity on a superphysical plane, of sight without eyes, hearing without ears, obtaining knowledge without physical apparatus. In default of any other explanation, the Theosophical hypothesis holds the field.

There is another class of facts: that of etheric and astral appearances, whether of living or dead persons, wraiths, apparitions, doubles, ghosts, etc., etc. Of course the omniscient person of the end of the nineteenth century will sniff with lofty disdain at the mention of such silly superstitions. But sniffs do not abolish facts, and it is a question of evidence. The weight of evidence is enormously on the side of such appearances, and in all ages of the world human testimony has borne witness to their reality. The inquirer whose demand for proof I have in view may well set to work to gather first-hand evidence on this head. Of course if he is afraid of being laughed at he had better leave the matter alone, but if he is robust enough to face the ridicule of the superior person he will be amazed at the evidence which he will collect from persons who have themselves come into contact with astral forms. "Illusions! hallucinations!" the superior person will say. But calling names settles nothing. Illusions to which the vast majority of the human race bears witness are at least worthy of study, if human testimony is to be taken as of any worth. There must be something which gives rise to this unanimity of testimony in all ages of the world, testimony which is found to-day among civilized people, amid railways and electric lights, as well as among barbarous races.

The testimony of millions of Spiritualists to the reality of etheric and astral forms cannot be left out of consideration. When all cases of fraud and imposture are discounted there remain phenomena that cannot be dismissed as fraudulent, and that can be examined by any persons who care to give time and trouble to the investigation. There is no necessity to employ a professional medium; a few friends, well known to each other, can carry on their search together; and it is not too much to say that any half-dozen persons, with a little patience and perseverance, may convince themselves of the existence of forces and of intelligences other than those of the physical plane. There is danger in this research to any emotional, nervous, and easily influenced natures, and it is well not to carry the investigations too far, for the reasons given on previous pages. But there is no readier way of breaking down the unbelief in the existence of anything outside the physical plane than trying a few experiments, and it is worth while to run some risk in order to effect this breaking down.

These are but hints as to lines that the inquirer may follow, so as to convince himself that there is a state of consciousness such as we label "astral". When he has collected evidence enough to make such a state probable to him, it will be time for him to be put in the way of serious study. For real investigation of the astral plane the student must develop in himself the necessary senses, and to make his knowledge available while he is in the body he must learn to transfer his consciousness to the astral plane without losing grip of the physical organism, so that he may impress on the physical brain the knowledge acquired during his astral voyagings. But for this he will need to be not a mere inquirer but a student, and he will require the aid and guidance of a teacher. As to the finding of that teacher, "when the pupil is ready the teacher is always there".

Further proofs of the existence of the astral plane are, at the present time, most easily found in the study of mesmeric and hypnotic phenomena. And here, ere passing to these, I am bound to put in a word of warning. The use of mesmerism and hypnotism is surrounded by danger. The publicity which attends on all scientific discoveries in the West has scattered broadcast knowledge which places within the reach of the criminally-disposed powers of the most terrible character, which may be used for the most damnable purposes. No good man or woman will use these powers, if he finds that he possesses them, save when he utilizes them purely for human service, without personal end in view, and when he is very sure that he is not by their means usurping control over the will and the actions of another human being. Unhappily the use of these forces is as open to the bad as to the good, and they may be, and are being, used to most nefarious ends. In view of these new dangers menacing individuals and society, each will do well to strengthen the habits of self-control and of concentration of thought and will, so as to encourage the positive mental attitude as opposed to the negative, and thus to oppose a sustained resistance to all influences coming from without. Our loose habits of thought, our lack of distinct and conscious purpose, lay us open to the attacks of the evil-minded hypnotizer, and that this is a real, not a fancied, danger has been already proved by cases that have brought the victims within the grasp of the criminal law. It may be hoped that ere long such hypnotic malpractices may be brought within the criminal code.

While thus in the attitude of caution and of self-defence, we may yet wisely study the experiments made public to the world, in our search for preliminary proofs of the existence of the astral plane. For here Western science is on the very verge of discovering some of those "powers" of which Theosophists have said so much, and we have the right to use in justification of our teachings all the facts with which that science may supply us.

Now, one of the most important classes of these facts is that of thoughts rendered visible as forms. A hypnotized person, after being awakened from trance and being apparently in normal possession of his senses, can be made to see any form conceived by the hypnotizer. No word need be spoken, no touch given ; it suffices that the hypnotizer should clearly image to himself some idea, and that idea becomes a visible and tangible object to the person under his control. This experiment may be tried in various ways ; while the patient is in trance, "suggestion" may be used ; that is, the operator may tell him that a bird is on his knee, and on awaking from the trance he will see the bird and will stroke it (*Etudes Cliniques sur la Grande Hystérie*, Richer, p. 645) ; or that he has a lampshade between his hands, and on awaking he will press his hands against it, feeling resistance in the empty air (*Animal Magnetism*, translated from Binet and Féré, p. 213) ; scores of these experiments may be read in Richer or in Binet and Féré. Similar results may be effected without "suggestion," by pure concentration of the thought ; I have seen a patient thus made to remove a ring from a person's finger, without word spoken or touch passing between hypnotizer and hypnotized.

The literature of mesmerism and hypnotism in English, French, and German is now very extensive, and it is open to every one. There may be sought the evidence of this creation of forms by thought and will, forms which, *on the astral plane*, are real and objective. Mesmerism and hypnotism set the intelligence free on this plane, and it works thereon without the hindrances normally imposed by the physical apparatus ; it can see and hear on that plane, and sees thoughts as things. Here, again, for real study, it is necessary to learn how thus to transfer the consciousness while retaining hold of the physical organism; but for preliminary inquiry it suffices to study others whose consciousness is artificially liberated without their own volition. This reality of thought-images on a superphysical plane is a fact of the very highest importance, especially in its bearing on reincarnation; but it is enough here to point to it as one of the facts which go to show the *prima facie* probability of the existence of such a plane.

Another class of facts deserving study is that which includes the phenomena of thought-transference, and here we reach the lower levels of the mental, or manasic, plane. The *Transactions of the Psychical Research Society* contain a large number of interesting experiments on this subject, and the possibility of the transference of thought from brain to brain without the use of words, or of any means of ordinary physical communication, is on the verge of general acceptance. And two persons, gifted with patience, may convince themselves of this possibility, if they care to devote to the effort sufficient time and perseverance. Let them agree to give, say, ten minutes daily to their experiment, and, fixing on the time, let each shut himself up alone, secure from interruption of any kind. Let one be the thought-projector, the other the thought-receiver, and it is safer to alternate these positions, in order to avoid the risk of one becoming permanently abnormally passive. Let the thought-projector concentrate himself on a definite thought and will to impress it on his friend; no other idea than the one must enter his mind; his thought must be concentrated on the one thing, "one-pointed" in the graphic language of Patanjali. The thought-receiver, on the other hand, must render his mind a blank, and must merely note the thoughts that drift into it. These he should put down as they appear, his only care being to remain passive, to reject nothing, to encourage nothing. The thought-projector, on his side, should keep a record of the ideas he tries to send, and at the end of six months the two records should be compared. Unless the persons are abnormally deficient in thought and will, some power of communication will by that time have been established between them ; and if they are at all psychic they will probably also have developed the power of seeing each other in the astral light.

It may be objected that such an experiment would be wearisome and monotonous. Granted. All first-hand investigations into natural laws and forces are wearisome and monotonous. That is why nearly every one prefers second-hand to first-hand knowledge; the "sublime patience of the investigator" is one of the rarest of gifts. Darwin would perform an apparently trivial experiment hundreds of times to substantiate one small fact; the supersensuous domains certainly do not need for their conquest less patience and less effort than the sensuous. Impatience never yet accomplished anything in the questioning of nature, and the would-be student must, at the very outset, show the tireless perseverance which can perish but cannot relinquish its hold.

Finally, let me advise the inquirer to keep his eyes open for new discoveries, especially in the sciences of electricity, physics, and chemistry. Let him read Professor Lodge's address to the British Association at Cardiff in the autumn of 1891 and Professor Crookes' address to the Society of Electrical Engineers in London in the following November. He will there find pregnant hints of the lines along which Western science is preparing to advance, and he will perchance begin to feel that there may be something in H. P. Blavatsky's statement that the Masters of Wisdom are preparing to give proofs that will substantiate the Secret Doctrine.

THE SEVEN PLANES AND THE PRINCIPLES FUNCTIONING THEREON.

Principle	Plane
7. x.	
6. x.	
5. Âtmâ. Spirit.	Spiritual.
4. Buddhi. Spiritual Soul.	Spiritual.
3. Manas. Human Soul.	Mental.
2. Kâma. Astral or Desire-Body.	Astral.
1. Prâna. Etheric Double. Dense Physical Body.	Physical.

ANOTHER DIVISION ACCORDING TO THE PRINCIPLES.

	7. Âtmâ.	Spiritual.
	6. Buddhi.	Spiritual.
	5. Higher Manas.	Mental.
Principles closely interwoven during earth-life. Sometimes called Higher Psychic Plane.	4. Lower Manas.	Mental.
Principles closely interwoven during earth-life. Sometimes called Higher Psychic Plane.	3. Kâma.	Astral.
	2. Prâna. Etheric Double.	Physical.
	1. Dense Physical Body.	Physical.

ANOTHER DIVISION, ALSO ACCORDING TO THE PRINCIPLES.

7. Âtmâ.	Spiritual.
6. Buddhi.	
5. Manas.	Mental.
4. Kâma.	Astral.
3. Prâna.	Physical.
2. Etheric Double.	
1. Dense Physical Body.	

These two latter divisions are matters of convenience in classification. The first diagram gives the planes themselves as they exist in nature.